P9-APP-142

# THE JOHN F. SLATER FUND

## A Nineteenth Century Affirmative Action for Negro Education

John E. Fisher

UNIVERSITY PRESS OF AMERICA

LANHAM • NEW YORK • LONDON

**University Press of America,® Inc.**

4720 Boston Way
Lanham, MD 20706

3 Henrietta Street
London WC2E 8LU England



Printed in the United States of America

**Library of Congress Cataloging in Publication Data**

Fisher, John E., 1926-
The John F. Slater Fund.

Bibliography: p.
Includes index.
1. John F. Slater Fund—History. 2. Afro-Americans—Scholarships, fellowships, etc.—United States.
3. Afro-Americans—Education—United States. I. Title.
LC2707.F57 1986 370'.8996073 86-24612
ISBN 0-8191-5714-7 (alk. paper)

Frontispiece:

From a portrait by Hubert Herkomer,

courtesy of the Library of Congress

All University Press of America books are produced on acid-free paper which exceeds the minimum standards set by the National Historical Publications and Records Commission.

To

*Nancy, Emmie,*
*John, and Steve*

John Fox Slater

# CONTENTS

# FOREWORD

The purpose of this volume is to examine the operations and principals of the John F. Slater Fund during the first ten years of the fund's existence, to explore the principals' motivations relative to the needs of black people, and to examine the applicability of the Slater model to the work of the Southern Education Foundation, the Slater Fund's successor agency and a contemporary affirmative action for black education.

Relying heavily upon correspondence from the Hayes Memorial, Fremont, Ohio, and the minutes of the Slater trustees, the study is interdisciplinary reflecting elements of history, management, biography, race relations, education, and philanthropy.

The author was originally attracted to the work of the agent, Atticus Greene Haygood of Georgia, in a graduate course in American social and cultural history. With later exposure to management theory and practice, the author perceived the managerial materialness of the interaction between trustees and between trustees and agent.

The Slater Fund harnessed the efforts of one of the most able and remarkable group of men that could have been assembled to accomplish a significant managerial task a hundred years ago. The trustees and Haygood, the agent, made the fund a model educational foundation in a number of ways, organizationally, procedurally, financially, in adapting to change and providing continuity, in its public relations, its division of tasks among specialists, monitoring and evaluation of the results of its initiatives, and its managerial elan.

I am indebted to Professor Henry Lee Swint of Vanderbilt University for introducing me to the fascinating field of Negro education in America and for encouraging my interest therein. A disciplined and innovative scholar, Professor Swint is a model teacher who adds excitement, humor, and urgency to the teaching of history.

I am indebted to librarians in the Library of Congress, Washington, D. C., and the Vanderbilt University Library,

Nashville, Tennessee. Thanks are also due to Leslie H. Fishel, Jr., Director of the Rutherford B. Hayes Presidential Center, Spiegel Grove, Fremont, Ohio, as well as the staffs of the Emory University Library, Atlanta, Georgia, the University of Virginia, Charlottesville, Virginia, and the New York Historical Society, New York City, for their research assistance.

To my wife, Nancy, my daughter, Mary Estelle Fisher-Lee, my sons, John and Stephen, my parents, Estelle Carr Fisher and the late Will Stratton Fisher, and my friend and teacher, Rhoda Lee Kennedy, I owe a special debt of gratitude.

John E. Fisher

Falls Church, Virginia

# INTRODUCTION

Modern American foundations date from the years immediately following the Civil War when unprecedentedly large American fortunes were amassed. Education was the primary beneficiary of the foundations, the Peabody (1867) and Slater (1882) funds being the earliest forerunners of even greater efforts which were to follow.

The foundations created by Andrew Carnegie and John D. Rockefeller were larger and broader in application than the two pioneer foundations. They built upon the same rule enunciated by the trustees of the Slater Fund, that people should be helped to help themselves. Those helped should show evidence of their diligence in self-improvement.[1]

In a number of ways, the John F. Slater Fund, established in 1882 to aid the education of blacks, was a model foundation (as was the Peabody Fund). Almost from its beginning, the Slater trust had a full-time salaried agent, Atticus Haygood of Georgia, who was the sense receptor of the corporation, travelling widely, observing the results of the fund's grants, recommending changes in grants, selling school officials on the desirability of providing industrial training, advising the trustees, and selling the aims of the fund to the general public. The fund provided full disclosure of its activities to the public. The board of trustees early recognized its responsibility to persuade the public to assist in the aims of Negro education.

Slater trustees actively participated in the fund's activities. They gave abundant evidence of being genuinely interested in their work as trustees, met at least annually to discuss their common objectives, and defined their responsibilities in bylaws. The trustees were representative geographically and vocationally, but not racially or sexually. Original trustees were residents of Ohio, the District of Columbia, Maryland, New York, Georgia, Massachusetts and Kentucky. They included a former president of the United States (R. B. Hayes), an active Chief Justice of the United States (M. R.

[1] The Commission on Foundations and Private Philanthropy, *Foundations, Private Giving and Public Policy* (Chicago: University of Chicago Press, 1970), pp. 93-94. Hereinafter cited as *Foundations, Private Giving and Public Policy.*

Waite), educators (D. C. Gilman of Johns Hopkins and J. P. Boyce of the Southern Baptist Theological Seminary), a retired banker who had become a full-time philanthropist (M. R. Jesup of New York), an active state governor (A. H. Colquitt of Georgia), a corporate official (W. E. Dodge of New York), a clergyman (Philips Brooks of Massachusetts), and a banker (J. A. Stewart of New York).

Trustees actively monitored and evaluated the fund's grants, so much that they repeatedly clashed with their paid agent, Haygood, insisting that he provide them with more and still more information which they believed they needed to properly administer the fund. From the beginning, they insisted on the self-help principle. Institutions aided were independently to raise amounts of money at least equivalent to the amounts received from the fund and to show evidence of growth. Students aided were to assist members of their race as evidence of being worthy of receipt of money from the fund.

There can be little doubt that the fund filled a significant national need. There was hardly any sector of American life in the 1880's more in need of assistance than education for blacks. The fund's resources were never sufficient to fill more than a small part of the need. But what was done was done well, and the attention which the fund's efforts focussed on the problem was much needed.

The fund's assets were managed remarkably well. In a period when the nation's economy was mercurial, fortunes won and lost rapidly, the fund suffered no losses of investments and received a steady albeit conservative return on its money. Further, the fund's resources were conserved by pooling its effort with that of the Peabody Fund after 1890. The funds each utilized the services of J. L. M. Curry, the Peabody agent who assumed Haygood's responsibilities in 1891. In 1914, when the Peabody Fund was dissolved, a portion of its assets ($346,797) was transferred to the Slater Fund.[2]

A foundation is an organization operated for a philanthropic purpose that has property and income of its own which is disbursed to achieve its goals. It is governed by trustees and has a paid staff—at

[2] The Peabody Education Fund's assets of $2.3 million were distributed three ways: 64.5 percent, or $1.5 million, went to endow George Peabody College for Teachers in Nashville; $474,000 was divided between fourteen colleges and universities in the southern states; and the balance went to the Slater Fund. Franklin Parker, "George Peabody's Influence on Southern Educational Philanthropy," *Tennessee Historical Quarterly* (March 1961), p. 72.

least an administrator. It serves as an intermediary between a donor (or donors) and the recipients of his or her philanthropy.

Prior to 1900, there were only ten foundations with assets of at least one million dollars.[3] Their total worth was $124 million. Contrast that to American foundations of the 1980's. In 1981, there were approximately 22,000 active grantmaking private foundations in the United States with assets of $51 billion and $4.1 billion in grants. The value of assets of American foundations declined 31 percent or $17.4 billion in constant dollars from 1972 to 1981, while their grants increased only 3 percent in constant dollars.[4]

The 1983 *Foundation Directory* lists only 26 foundations that were established prior to 1900. The 1950's was the decade of greatest foundation growth when 35 percent of all currently listed foundations were established.[5]

In 1982, 42.5 percent of all grant dollars went to educational institutions, primarily private universities and colleges. Direct service agencies (including social service agencies, boy and girl scouts, recreational agencies, employment services) received 18.5 percent of grant dollars, a growing proportion. Hospitals and medical care facilities received 9.1 percent, a diminishing amount. Fellowships and scholarships accounted for 5.5 percent of awards.[6]

Several American foundations with only modest endowments to begin with have grown to be the largest. The Ford Foundation, started in 1936 to support the local charities of the Ford family, became, in the late 1940's following the deaths of Henry and Edsel Ford, the largest of all private foundations with a multibillion dollar endowment.

In late 1971, the Robert Wood Johnson Foundation of New Jersey became the second largest when it was given assets of over a billion dollars by the will of its founder.[7] The Ford Foundation has about $2.6 billion in assets and annual grants of about $89.1 million. The Robert Wood Johnson Foundation has assets of $1.4 billion and grants of $42.0 million.[8]

[3] Arnold J. Kurcher, *The Management of American Foundations* (New York: New York University Press, 1972), pp. 7-8, Hereinafter cited as *Management of American Foundations.*

[4] Loren Renz (ed.), *The Foundation Directory* (9th ed.; New York: The Foundation Center, 1983), p. xvii. Hereinafter cited as *Foundation Directory.*

[5] *Ibid.,* p. xv.

[6] *Ibid.,* pp. xxv-xxvi.

[7] *Management of American Foundations,* pp. 19-20.

[8] *Foundation Directory,* p. xvi.

The founder and original trustees of the John F. Slater Fund could hardly have conceived of administering those amounts in their relatively modest operation. In 1881, however, a one million dollar trust was not an inconsiderable fund. The Slater Fund began with $1 million, the Peabody Educational Fund with $2 million.

In his study of large contemporary foundations (published in 1972), Merrimon Cunninggim found that the Ford Foundation, with 9.7 percent, had the highest rate of expenditures ($282.7 million) as a percentage of the market value of its assets ($2.9 billion). The rate of expenditure of the Ford Foundation most recently reported was 0.3 percent, a sharp drop indeed. By contrast, the rate for the Andrew W. Mellon Foundation, the nation's seventh largest, was much larger, 7.3 percent, on grants of $58.4 million out of assets of $0.8 billion. In the Cunninggim survey, only three foundations, Ford, Commonwealth, and Danforth, exceeded a 6 percent payout figure.[9] The Slater Fund during its first nine years of operation expended a conservative 3.2 percent annual average and never exceeded 4.1 percent. Such were the limitations on its returns on investments.

The amount of Slater grants was small, only $321,991 in the period 1882-1891. Yet Slater aid was much sought after in a period when schools for blacks in the South primarily looked for financial aid to the states, the American Missionary Association (supported primarily by Congregational churches), the Freedman's Aid Society of the Methodist Episcopal Church, and the American Baptist Home Mission Society. And the Slater experience was influential in later and better endowed educational efforts in the twentieth century.

In terms of foundation management, only one-fifth of all U. S. foundations had any paid staff at all, including secretaries, according to a study by the Commission on Foundations and Private Philanthropy. Only 5 percent had any full-time salaried staff.

The median administrative overhead for all foundations was 2.9 percent, according to the commission's findings. The Slater Fund's median overhead (1882-91) was 14.5 percent, a figure which may not be altogether unfavorable considering the comparatively small size of each Slater grant. Note the size of Slater grants in Appendix G.

[9] Merrimon Cunninggim, *Private Money and Public Service* (New York: McGraw-Hill, 1972), pp. 65-67, 71. See also *Foundation Directory*, p. xvi.

In almost two-fifths of U. S. foundations, board members play so small a role in the determination of grants as to be virtually invisible. The boards of nine percent of the foundations never meet; the trustees of 33 percent meet once a year or less, and 15 percent meet for one hour or less annually. These represent the boards of small foundations principally. A few of the largest foundations have quarterly and sometimes monthly board meetings of a day or two in length.

Trustees of the larger foundations typically are not geographically representative. Most are residents of the New England-Middle Atlantic region. Half of the trustees of the 25 largest trusts attended Ivy League schools, and about two-thirds have business, banking, or legal backgrounds. Few are women, youthful, or black.

Forty-one percent of American foundations never take steps to monitor the use or results of their grants. This is more often the case with small rather than large foundations. Most philanthropic trusts are involved in simply conceiving and awarding grants rather than evaluating them for results in terms of success or failure, learning from them, and disseminating reports of results to interested parties.[10]

The Federal Tax Reform Act of 1969 (P. L. 91-172) included a number of measures which restricted the activities of foundations. Provisions were included to discourage speculative investments, to require the equivalent of six percent of each foundation's assets to be distributed annually (The Economic Recovery Tax Act of 1981 changed the payout requirement to 5 percent of market value of assets), and to require the issuance of a public report annually.[11] Except for the requirement to distribute assets at an annual six (changed to five) percent rate, the Slater trustees were doing this in the 1880's.

Duties of trustees vary widely among foundations. Trustees may make policy, concern themselves with administrative details, make decisions about investments and expenditures, review requests for grants, and appraise the results of grants. They may involve themselves with keeping the public informed on the foundation's activities. Arnold J. Zurcher observed that the degree of dedication and intellectual level of the board members will largely determine the quality of a foundation's program. Foundations, he believes,

[10] *Foundations, Private Giving and Public Policy,* pp. 87-92.

[11] Maxwell S. Stewart, "The Big Foundations," *Public Affairs Pamphlet* No. 500 (November 1973), p. 20. See also *Foundation Directory,* p. ix.

should seek to secure trustees with exceptional capabilities and to engage their interests by making their roles meaningful and accordingly useful.

It is beneficial to have an honest and trusting relationship between trustees and paid staff, to retire older trustees in order to avoid inflexibility, to appoint trustees who represent different professions, social strata, and geographical origins. Foundation boards usually have no blacks, women, social workers, clerics, active scientists, scholars, or engineers.

It is desirable that board meetings last long enough, at least two or three days, to permit time for trustees to become familiar with issues confronting them, and to confer with fellow trustees and staff members relative to issues they face. Staff members should have sufficient discretion in committing the fund to specific grants so as to free trustees from being immersed in minutia and give trustees time to concentrate on policy.

Compensation of trustees should be based on the reasonable worth of the service rendered. Compensation permits the appointment and acceptance of trusteeships by clerics, teachers, social workers, and others who without pay could not devote time to the task.[12]

The Peabody Education Fund, founded in 1867, set a precedent of focusing public attention on the educational needs of the people of the southern states fifteen years before the Slater Fund was started. George Peabody had sought publicity for his greatest philanthropy by appointing trustees of national stature and designing their meetings as significant public events. The Peabody trustees began the practice of meeting at the great hostelry of the day, the Fifth Avenue Hotel in New York City. Their meetings were widely noted in the press around the country. The Slater trustees followed the lead of the Peabody Fund in this as well as other respects. Several of them were Peabody trustees before they became Slater trustees.

Slater trustees were among those who met early in 1902 to begin the work of the General Education Board, the Rockefeller-backed foundation which has had a profound effect on southern life in the twentieth century. Those attending the first meetings of the board were Messrs. John D. Rockefeller, Jr., Frederick T. Gates, William

[12] *Management of American Foundations,* pp. 32, 35.

H. Baldwin, Jr., J. L. M. Curry, Robert C. Ogden, Daniel C. Gilman, Walter Hines Page, Albert Shaw, Wallace Buttrick, and Morris K. Jesup.[13] The experience of the Slater board was felt well outside the narrow confines of the inner workings of the board itself. Half of the men were Slater trustees who met to organize the General Education Board in January and February of 1902.

What about the quality of the annual and special reports the Slater board required of aided institutions? Were they mere listings? Or sermons? Did they describe the application of grants in detail? Did they explain school policy? Were they self-serving? Or confusing? Did they attempt to measure the success or failure of specific grants?

Admittedly, evaluation criteria are difficult to develop and apply. Slater trustees required systematic reporting by recipients of grants, including detailed financial reports. A typical report from a school aided with Slater money provided the name of the chief executive officer—principal or president; the date the school was organized; under whose auspices it was operated; the value of its property; the number of officers, teachers, and pupils; the amount of the Slater appropriation and its use, viz.:

| | |
|---|---|
| Salaries of instructors | $904.00 |
| Materials for greenhouse | 100.00 |
| Materials for new shop | 250.00 |
| Tools and printing materials | 46.00 |
| Total | $1,300.00 |

There followed a narrative of highlights of the school year or an appreciation of the work which the Slater appropriation permitted: A new hall completed and furnished providing an improved kitchen, printing, and serving rooms; the number of students accommodated in the cooking and housekeeping department; the workload capacity of the laundry operated by students; a new nursing course made possible which is conducted by a graduate of the Massachusetts General Hospital; reaction of local newspapers to school developments and programs; news of graduates, viz., one has recently departed for the Congo as a missionary; another is principal of a school in Arkansas.

The foregoing is the style initiated by Haygood, the first Slater agent, which was essentially unchanged by his successors, Curry and

[13] Abraham Flexner, *Funds and Foundations* (New York: Harper & Brothers, 1952), p. 29.

Buttrick. Narratives tended to be lengthier and more uniform under the latter two.

In 1896, George W. Hubbard, dean of Meharry Medical College in Nashville reported to the Slater trustees on the state of the health of blacks in the South. He stated that the death rate among blacks in the southern states was about twice as high as that for whites, owing to ignorance of the "laws of health" and lack of proper care when sick from preventable diseases. He stated that a large increase in the number of colored physicians was urgently needed. He observed that in 1895 there were only about 385 "regularly educated" black physicians to care for about 7 million Negroes, or one physician for about 20,000 people. In Nashville, where he said there was probably a greater number of black physicians in proportion to the population than anywhere else, the death rate had declined nearly 40 percent during the last 20 years. Thus he indicated the great value of increasing educational opportunities for prospective black physicians.

On a hopeful note, he asserted that there had been cordial professional relations between Meharry alumni and white physicians which was helping to establish "mutual kindness and good-will between the two races," doubtless the sort of observation that individuals interested in progressive philanthropy, such as the Slater trustees, liked to hear.[14]

The influence of Slater work was realized in the lives of student recipients who later distinguished themselves either locally or on a broader stage. W. E. B. DuBois wrote to Daniel C. Gilman, president of the Slater trustees following the death of Rutherford B. Hayes in 1893. Assuring Gilman that he would strive to show results stemming from his Slater grant, he expressed his appreciation and paid tribute to "the memory of him, your late head [Hayes], through whose initiative my case was brought before you." Dubois wrote of Hayes' "tireless energy and singleheartedness for the interests of my Race, [which] God has at last crowned."[15]

Benjamin Brawley, writing in 1923 of the Slater Fund's early efforts for industrial education, quoted DuBois to the effect that the "singularly wise administration" of the Slater trust was "perhaps the greatest single impulse toward the economic emancipation of the

[14] *Proceedings,* Slater Trustees (1896), pp. 16, 17.

[15] W. E. B. DuBois to D. C. Gilman, undated, in Louis D. Rubin, Jr. (ed.) *Teach the Freeman: The Correspondence of Rutherford B. Hayes and the Slater Fund for Negro Education* (Baton Rouge: Louisiana State University Press, 1959), Vol. II, p. 281.

Negro."[16] This from the pre-eminent protagonist of the view that blacks should not be suppressed as a provider of cheap labor!

[16] Benjamin Brawley, "Early Efforts for Industrial Education," The Trustees of the John F. Slater Fund, *Occasional Papers,* No. 22 (1923), p. 14.

# Chapter 1

# Origins of the Slater Fund

Former U. S. President Rutherford B. Hayes went to New York City in early October, 1881, to have his portrait painted for the Harvard Law School and to attend a meeting of the trustees of the Peabody Education Fund. Leonard Bacon, John F. Slater's pastor, visited Hayes in his suite in the Fifth Avenue Hotel on October 9. Bacon carried with him a letter of recommendation from Morrison R. Waite, Chief Justice of the United States. He came to see Hayes at Slater's behest to discuss the organization of an educational foundation to aid Negroes.[1]

During November and December of 1881, Atticus Haygood, a Methodist clergyman from Georgia, travelled through southern New England delivering a speech titled, "The New South From A Southern Standpoint."[2] In his speech, he attempted to dissociate in the minds of his hearers white southerners from slavery. He described the progress of the freedmen, the work of northern philanthropy in the southern states, and expressed hope for national unity, a missing ingredient at that time.[3]

While Haygood's speaking tour was in progress, and indeed prior to it, John F. Slater's plans for establishing a fund for the benefit of Negro education were proceeding. Bacon sent a request to Haygood to meet him and Slater in Norwich, Connecticut, "on business of importance to southern education." Their meeting took place on

[1] Louis D. Rubin, Jr. (ed.), *Teach the Freeman: The Correspondence of Rutherford B. Hayes and the Slater Fund for Negro Education* (Baton Rouge: Louisiana State University Press, 1959), Vol. I, pp. xiii-xv. Hereinafter cited as Rubin, *Teach the Freeman.*

[2] Marion L. Smith, "Atticus Greene Haygood: Christian Educator" (Unpublished Ph. D. Dissertation: Yale University, 1929), p. 334. Hereinafter cited as Smith, "Haygood." The speech was delivered in Tremont Temple, Boston, Massachusetts, at noon Monday, December 12, 1881. It was delivered in substance in fifteen other cities and towns of New England.

[3] *Wesleyan Christian Advocate,* December 17, 1881.

December 21. Later Bacon wrote to Hayes that "Mr. Slater . . . was much pleased with Dr. Haygood (he *is* a capital gentleman)."[4]

A former pastor of Slater's, S. H. Howe, said that Moses Pierce, a neighbor, had influenced Slater to make his gift to Negro education.[5] It was Slater's habit to spend four evenings each week in conversation with Pierce.[6] The latter was a trustee of Hampton Institute in Virginia and a benefactor of schools established to aid blacks.[7] He shared his interest in education for blacks with Slater.

One Sunday, Leonard Bacon delivered a sermon on the opportunity of advancing human welfare by the proper use of wealth. Slater was in the congregation. At the close of the sermon, Slater informed Bacon that he had decided to contribute a million dollars for Negro education.[8]

Atticus Haygood, the Georgia clergyman, took an early interest in the new Slater trust. Having been consulted in December about its establishment, he wrote to Bacon that "the whole question of the Negroes and their future affects me profoundly." Even before the fund was organized, Haygood sought employment with it. He wrote to Bacon saying he thought he could give the fund the leadership it would need. He said that he was "credited with common sense and business methods" as well as "good knowledge of men." He was a hard worker who knew the South and its people. He was reconciled to the results of the Civil War and felt great interest in the welfare of Negroes. He thought that his experience as president of Emory College (1875-1885) would be valuable to him in the Slater work. He felt that he had the confidence of both whites and blacks in the South. He added: "I am in friendly correspondence with the leading Bishops of the Colored churches."[9]

The John F. Slater Fund was organized in New York by its board of trustees and granted a charter of incorporation by the state on April 28, 1882.[10] The first meeting of the trustees was held at the

[4] L. W. Bacon to R. B. Hayes, December 26, 1881. Hayes MSS., Rutherford B. Hayes Presidential Center, Spiegel Grove, Fremont, Ohio. Hereinafter cited as Hayes MSS..

[5] Smith, "Haygood," p. 330.

[6] Will W. Alexander, "The Slater and Jeanes Funds, An Educator's Approach to a Difficult Social Problem," The Trustees of the John F. Slater Fund, *Occasional Papers,* No. 28 (1934), p. 4. Hereinafter cited as Alexander, "The Slater and Jeanes Funds."

[7] Smith, "Haygood," p. 330.

[8] Alexander, "The Slater and Jeanes Funds," p. 4.

[9] A. G. Haygood to L. W. Bacon, January 25, 1882, Hayes MSS..

[10] "Organization of the Trustees of the John F. Slater Fund for the Education of Freedmen," The Trustees of the John F. Slater Fund (1882), pp. 11, 12. Hereinafter cited as "Organization of the Trustees."

office of Morris K. Jesup, 52 William Street, New York City, at which time bylaws were approved and the organization of the board completed. Only two trustees (Phillips Brooks and William E. Dodge) were absent from the first meeting.

The trustees provided that the general agent of the fund, in connection with the trustees' executive committee would be charged with the duty of carrying out the designs of the trust under instructions which would be given by the board. The executive committee, in conjunction with the general agent, likewise was charged with the duty of carrying out the resolutions and orders of the board.

One of the adopted bylaws provided for the appointment at each annual meeting of both a finance and an executive committee. Another specified that the annual meeting of the board would be held "at such place in the City of New York as shall be designated by the Board, or the President, on the first Thursday following the first Wednesday of October in each year."[11]

Slater's instructions to the trustees left a great deal to the discretion of the board.[12] He specified that the intent of the fund was to aid in the Christian education of Negroes and indicated that he wished the training of teachers to be encouraged. The charter of the fund stipulated that trustees were to number no more than twelve and not less than nine. Slater designated Rutherford B. Hayes the first president of the board. In order that the capital of the fund should remain intact, Slater specified that a part of the income should be invested if the capital fell below its original amount. If the fund were no longer needed in its initial form at the end of thirty-three years, three-fourths of the trustees might cause the capital to be used for the establishment of foundations subsidiary to the colleges and universities which would help poor Negro students. The trust should be administered in no "partisan, sectional, or sectarian spirit." The trustees were to be chosen from men "distinguished either by honorable success in business, or by services to literature, education, religion, or the State."

Slater's letter of instructions to the trustees was put in final form by Simeon Eben Baldwin, professor of law at Yale University, later governor of Connecticut and Chief Justice of the Connecticut supreme court.[13]

[11] By-Laws of the Slater Trustees Adopted May 18, 1882. The Slater Trustees *Proceedings* (1883), p. 26.

[12] The letter of the founder to the trustees is found in Appendix H.

[13] L. W. Bacon to R. B. Hayes, February 6, 1882, Hayes MSS..

The tax advantages of establishing foundations which exist for today's philanthropists did not exist in 1882 when the federal government's principal source of revenue was customs. Rather than giving directly to a school or individual, Slater's transfer of assets to the foundation provided that the funds would be spent upon the advice of the appointed trustees. In this way, Slater shared the responsibility for disposition of the funds and received what he hoped would be expert advice in how the money could be best distributed.

Slater (who was 67 in 1882), by establishing the foundation, assured that his philanthropy would be continued after his death. He recognized that the needs of Negro education would change with the passage of time. Thus he established the foundation in the knowledge that it provided flexibility in aid to recipients in response to changing needs.

The foundation, with its trustees and general agent, provided insulation for Slater from involvement with direct appeals for contributions. And, of course, the fund, bearing the name of John F. Slater, gave Slater a degree of status and distinction while he lived and assured the perpetuation of his name until the fund was merged in 1937 into the Southern Education Foundation.

Although the fund was chartered by the State of New York, Leonard Bacon had misgivings and wrote to Hayes that, considering the national nature of the foundation, it might be appropriate to seek incorporation by special act of Congress. This would secure the fund against trouble from state legislation. "It might happen at some future time," he thought, "that a Comm. or N. Y. Legislature would cease to feel a special friendliness toward a Corp. spending its whole income in distant states."[14]

Writing to Hayes, J. L. M. Curry, Peabody trustee and Harvard classmate of Hayes, raised the issue of the trustees being restricted to aiding sectarian schools: ". . . Our public schools do not give 'Christian' education, even when the Bible is used in them. . . ," he wrote.[15] Hayes queried Bacon regarding this point, and Bacon replied that "Mr. Slater's Boston Unitarian friends objected to it [the words, 'Christian education'] on the ground that it might devote the fund to theological and sectarian competitions." But Slater believed that, in the sense which he intended, the common schools of

[14] *Ibid.*, October 28, 1881, Hayes MSS..

[15] J. L. M. Curry to R. B. Hayes, July 8, 1882, Hayes MSS..

Massachusetts and Connecticut taught "Christian education," that is, "it is leavened with a predominantly and salutary Christian influence."[16]

The first Slater trustees were men who had achieved prominence in a number of vocations. They were chosen by the founder,[17] who undoubtedly wanted his pastor, Leonard W. Bacon, to be a trustee also. But since Bacon was an outspoken theological maverick, he was too controversial (or so it was believed) to serve.[18] Bacon had both theological and medical degrees from Yale and served both Congregational and Presbyterian pastorates. He was a prolific writer, polemical, a controversialist who made enemies, and was characterized as "a gadfly to Congregationalists."

Hayes was designated president of the board by Slater. The trustees elected Morrison R. Waite, vice president, Daniel C. Gilman, secretary, and Morris K. Jesup, treasurer.[19] A number of men were suggested for the position of general agent of the trustees, Atticus Haygood, the Georgian who was already making a name for himself as a friend of the freedmen, being among the first. As early as February 1882, Slater's pastor, Leonard Bacon, wrote from Norwich, Connecticut, to Hayes that "this is my time to do a little lobbying for my candidate, Dr. Haygood, author of 'Our Brother in Black'." He believed that Haygood could be had as agent for the fund for at least two or three years and commended "the consideration of his qualifications to the future trustees."[20]

Other candidates for the position included Hamilton Wilcox Pierson, a Presbyterian clergyman and author, a graduate of Yale who had travelled extensively through the South before the Civil War as an agent for the American Tract Society and had organized schools for Negroes both during and after the war.[21] Still another possibility for the position was Lewis H. Steiner, a scientist and teacher who was a trustee of Hampton Institute.[22]

In July 1882, J. L. M. Curry, agent of the Peabody Education Fund, who later filled a similar position with the Slater Fund, wrote

[16] L. W. Bacon to R. B. Hayes, July 21, 1882, Hayes MSS..

[17] John F. Butler, "An Historical Account of the John F. Slater Fund and the Anna T. Jeanes Foundation," (Unpublished Ed. D. Thesis: University of California, 1931), p. 88. Hereinafter cited as Butler, "An Historical Account."

[18] Rubin, *Teach the Freeman,* Vol. I, p. xix.

[19] "Organization of the Trustees," p. 17.

[20] L. W. Bacon to R. B. Hayes, February 6, 1882, Hayes MSS..

[21] William Baker to M. R. Waite, April 27, 1882, Hayes MSS..

[22] D. C. Gilman to R. B. Hayes, June 30, 1882, Hayes MSS..

to Hayes that the Slater agent "should be intelligently and boldly, but not fanatically, a friend of the negroes, anxious for their moral and intellectual elevation and a believer in the possibilities of 'the race.' " Further, "he should be patient, prudent, full of tact, firm, conciliatory, able to manage men, to address assemblies, and an unalterable advocate of free schools." Curry believed that the agent's job would be "no bed of roses," therefore he would distrust anyone who "self-reliantly" sought the position.[23]

Apparently Curry did not know that Haygood was seeking the position (rather self reliantly) since nine days later he wrote again to Hayes, endorsing Haygood for the agency. He explained that he did not know Haygood personally, but he was sure that he would make a "very efficient agent." He remarked that Haygood "is a broad and catholic Christian & patriot and his 'Our Brother in Black' shows courage, ability, and right opinions on the Negro Problem."[24]

Governor Colquitt of Georgia also endorsed Haygood and wrote to Hayes that he was "glad to say that there is a prospect of securing the services of Dr. Haygood . . . if you desire him. I shall consider ourselves fortunate if we can do this."[25] This communication was a result of a meeting which Colquitt and Bishop George F. Pierce had with Haygood at which time Haygood was advised to accept the position."[26]

The correspondence of the Slater trustees indicates that Hayes, Boyce, Gilman, Dodge, and Will Slater, as well as John F. Slater and Leonard Bacon endorsed Haygood for the job. Some years later, J. L. M. Curry asserted that Slater had determined to secure Haygood as the first general agent because it was Haygood's book, *Our Brother in Black,* which had so strongly influenced the making of the gift.[27]

At the Slater board's second meeting, held in the Fifth Avenue Hotel, New York City's finest hostelry on the northwest corner of Fifth Avenue at Twenty-Third Street, October 5 and 7, 1882, the executive committee was unanimously authorized to tender Haygood the appointment as agent. The trustees, again with only Brooks and Dodge absent, requested the general agent to recommend a plan of operations calling his attention to the following suggestions:

[23] J. L. M. Curry to R. B. Hayes, July 6, 1882, Hayes MSS..

[24] *Ibid.,* July 17, 1882, Hayes MSS..

[25] A. H. Colquitt to R. B. Hayes, July 12, 1882, Hayes MSS..

[26] A. G. Haygood, "A Long and Weary March," Nashville *Christian Advocate,* May 9, 1891.

[27] Butler, "An Historical Account," p. 89.

1. The fund should assist promising youth.
2. Scholarships should provide only partial support to their beneficiaries.
3. A record should be kept of the progress of students aided after they leave school so that the results of the fund's assistance may be evaluated.
4. Aided scholars shall, insofar as practicable, receive manual as well as mental and moral instruction.
5. Recipients of Slater aid should be encouraged to return to their schools funds in the amount of the aid they received.
6. Special assistance should be given worthy students.
7. Inquiry should be made as to whether the fund should aid schools not now providing adequate instruction.[28]

The trustees' preoccupation with student aid was short-lived. Through the years it never exceeded $550 annually and was discontinued altogether after 1891.

Haygood was delighted with his election to the agency. His work was to be on a part-time basis, since he retained his connection with Emory College. But he felt that he would be able to do the work well. He confidently explained to Hayes: "I only say what everybody hereabouts knows—I can do more work than the majority of men and have done it for twenty years." Haygood went on to say that he had only two classes at Emory and that they could be provided for when it was necessary for him to be absent. He cited the year 1881 when he was "seven full weeks North in college time. . . . I was in Nashville a full month at our General Conference this year. I can give as much time to the Slater Fund as it may require."[29]

On October 14, 1882, Hayes wrote Gilman that Haygood had accepted the agency. "All things seem well with us," he said. Gilman expressed gratification in reply.[30] Attacks, however, were made upon Haygood who had declined the office of bishop in his church in May and became Slater agent five months later. He was accused of being bought by a $3,000 salary.[31]

Late in October, before returning home, Haygood addressed the American Missionary Association meeting in Cleveland, Ohio, on "The Negro A Citizen." In his speech he emphasized the desirability

[28] "Organization of the Trustees," pp. 19-20.
[29] A. G. Haygood to R. B. Hayes, October 11, 1882, Hayes MSS..
[30] R. B. Hayes to D. C. Gilman, October 14, 1882; D. C. Gilman to R. B. Hayes, October 17, 1882, Hayes MSS..
[31] Smith, "Haygood," pp. 55-57.

of educating the freedmen for citizenship and reviewed some of the work which the Association had done for Negroes. He spoke of the danger of placing the ballot in the hands of people unprepared to vote, and endorsed federal aid for primary education, an endorsement he was not prepared to make when he discussed the topic in his book, *Our Brother In Black* (1881). He believed, however, that higher education should have a Christian orientation and that the state could not do the work as well as the church. Haygood also spoke of some of the difficulties encountered by southern whites since the Civil War and declared that the poverty of the section had kept southern whites from doing more for Negroes. In conclusion he injected the theme of national unity into his speech. "Men and brethren," he declared, "it is time to have done with 1860-65."[32]

Meanwhile, the trustees' responsibility for the fund's investments was not neglected. Hayes wrote to Jesup about the favorable condition of the New Albany, Louisville, and Chicago Railroad, one of the lines whose bonds were purchased by Slater before he relinquished control of his assets to the trustees. Hayes wrote: "I trust that in future no bonds will be purchased except those of strictly first-class RR's whose payments of dividends are regularly made. . . ." Hayes anticipated hard times frequently during the lifetime of the trust, "when at least three-fourths of all the RR's of the country will fail to pay their interest." He hoped that Slater investments would be made exclusively in the securities of the remaining fourth which would continue to pay. "The desire to have a good income," he said, "wrecks a host of Trust funds at every recurring financial panic. Let us avoid this sure road to ruin."[33]

In December 1882, Morris Jesup, acting for the trustees, sold the fund's Marietta and Cleveland Railroad bonds at par and interest to Major General Wager Swayne, counsel for several railroad and telegraph companies in New York.[34] Less than a year and a half later, the Marietta and Cleveland Railroad failed in the panic of May 5-7, 1884.[35]

On December 6, 1882, Haygood wrote enthusiastically to Hayes of new progress made in the field of Negro education. The previous

[32] The address is found in A. G. Haygood, *Sermons and Speeches* (Nashville: Southern Methodist Publishing House, 1883), pp. 373-391.

[33] R. B. Hayes to M. K. Jesup, November 23, 1882, Hayes MSS..

[34] M. R. Waite to R. B. Hayes, January 1, 1883, Hayes MSS.. Waite mistakenly referred to the railroad as the Marietta and Cincinnati.

[35] Rubin, *Teach the Freeman,* Vol. I, p. 108.

May, the General Conference of the Methodist Episcopal Church, South, passed a resolution for the establishment of a school for blacks. Specifically the conference had provided for the appointment of a commissioner of education who would solicit donations, subscriptions, and bequests for the school. Editorials in the *Wesleyan Christian Advocate* (Macon, Georgia) during the years 1879-82 when Haygood was editor were instrumental in establishing the school which was to be known as Paine Institute and to be located in Augusta, Georgia.[36] The school became the joint responsibility of the Methodist Episcopal Church, South, and the Colored Methodist Episcopal Church, an offspring of the former church.

As early as September 1878, the Nashville *Christian Adovcate* commented editorially on the need for a school in which the ministers of the CME Church might be educated. It commended the enterprise to the "sympathy and support of thinking Christian men and women."[37]

The commissioner of education presented his first report on December 2, 1882, and asked Bishop George F. Pierce to appoint Morgan Callaway to the presidency of Paine Institute.[38] Callaway was vice president of Emory College and Professor of English Language and Literature. Haygood explained that, when a suitable man was sought for the head of the school. Callaway came "forward and proposed to take this Negro college . . . & give his life to it. It has made simply a tremendous impression on our people." Haygood declared that Callaway was of a long line of aristocratic slave-owners, was a native of Georgia, and an officer who served with distinction in the war. He had the "absolute confidence of our people." Haygood remarked that this was the "first case of the kind; it will not be the last. It marks the beginning of a new chapter in the history of . . . our section."[39]

Although he later rejoiced that leading white citizens were willing to serve on the board of trustees with Negroes,[40] response to pleas for financial support of the school was poor (doubtless owing at least in part to the South's poverty), although two years later it was sufficient for the formal opening of the institution which survives a hundred years later.

[36] Smith, "Haygood," pp. 310-313.
[37] Nashville *Christian Advocate,* September 7, 1878.
[38] *Ibid.,* December 23, 1882.
[39] A. G. Haygood to R. B. Hayes, December 6, 1882, Hayes MSS..
[40] *Ibid.,* January 3, 1883, Hayes MSS..

# Chapter 2

# Dramatis Personae: Founder, Trustees, and Agent (1882–1891)

The John F. Slater Fund was set in motion during the heyday of the "robber barons" who economically dominated the period from the Civil War to the Great Depression of the 1930's, a period when unprecedentedly large fortunes were made by a few while most people lived lives of economic want in terms of American economic standards of the late twentieth century. In the period of which we write, the "Golden Age" of the American economy was a long way off. Prosperity was enjoyed by a miniscule portion of the population. But even for the fortunate few, prosperity was often a sometime thing, so great were the risks and mercurial the economy.

Further, the fortunes accrued by philanthropists with whom we will become acquainted in these pages, men like Slater and George Peabody, William E. Dodge and Morris K. Jesup, were small by comparison with those of the Rockefellers and Carnegies. The men who by and large made up the prime movers of the Slater Fund in the beginning were acculturated to an early nineteenth century mercantile mentality and a degree of civility which was uncommon to the most acquisitive people of means of their time.[1]

Except for the southerners amongst them, most of the Slater Fund figures were from New England (or had New England antecedents). Those who amassed fortunes as industrialists had gone to work as teenagers, one (Jesup) as early as age twelve. Those

[1] In the preparation of sketches of people connected with the Slater trust which are found on the following pages, the following biographical dictionaries have been consulted:

*Appleton's Cyclopedia of American Biography* (8 vols., New York, 1887-1889, 1900).
*Dictionary of American Biography* (22 vols., 7 supplements, New York, 1928-1981).
*National Cyclopedia of American Biography* (75 vols., New York, 1898-1984).

who had consuming pecuniary passions had been tempered by the time they became associated with the Slater Fund and were involved in the performance of good works.

Again with respect to those from the North, occupationally, five (the two Slaters, the two Dodges, and Jesup) were industrialists, of whom three (Jesup, the younger Slater and Dodge) might be termed industrialist-philanthropists. Of course, W. E. Dodge, Jr. and William Slater were second generation industrialists who inherited their industrial interests. The third (Jesup) was a merchant-industrialist, then a banker. He retired from active involvement in business in his fifties and thereafter devoted himself almost exclusively to philanthropy.

Among the northerners, there were two clerics (Brooks and Potter), both of whom were Episcopalians who were or became bishops. Three (Chief Justices Fuller and Waite and former President Hayes) were lawyers of whom one (Hayes) might be termed a lawyer-politician. One (Stewart) was a banker (Of course, Jesup was a merchant-industrialist-banker) and one an educator (Gilman). Only Potter and Gilman had any sort of reputation for scholarship, although Gilman's reputation rested more on being a pioneering university administrator than on scholarship, and Potter's, more on being an innovative and broad-minded ecclesiastic.Of those who were identified strongly with religious denominations, all were either Congregationalists, Episcopalians, or Presbyterians. On the other hand, Hayes, following his marriage, gave undivided support to the Methodist Episcopal Church whilst being a member of no church.

Four of the five from the South were not only educators, but scholarly as well. They included Boyce, Broadus, Curry, and Haygood. They published original scholarly works which were regarded by their contemporaries as exemplary. The fifth southerner (Colquitt) was a laywer-politician. The southerners were either Baptists or Methodists. All the educators were ordained; Colquitt was a lay preacher. Three of the southerners (Boyce, Colquitt and Curry) earned college degrees in the North. All five were college educated. As a group, they were sons of families which had prospered and attained advantages and a degree of gentility before they were born. Educationally, the same could be said to characterize those from the North, although William E. Dodge, Sr., Morris Jesup, and the founder, John F. Slater, had common school educations.

Among the trustees, three (Fuller, Hayes, and Curry) supplemented their AB degrees by attendance at law schools. Three (Boyce, Brooks, and Potter) were graduates of theological seminaries, one (Potter) without prior college training. Gilman supplemented his college course with advanced study.

## John Fox Slater

John Fox Slater chose the trustees and Haygood, the agent, with advice and counsel from his associates. Morris Jesup's biographer, William Adams Brown, stated that Slater came to Jesup's office to consult with his friend about the best way to accomplish his purpose.[2]

When he established the fund, Slater was 67 years of age and within two years of his death. Prior to this time, Slater had shown little interest in philanthropy other than to help found and endow the Norwich (Connecticut) Free Academy in 1868. And he is reported to have contributed liberally to the Park Congregational Church in Norwich.

Slater was the son of John Slater who emigrated from England about 1804. He had knowledge of machinery used to make yarns and cloth. His brother, Samuel Slater, uncle to John Fox, established the first cotton mill in the United States. He was called the "father of American manufactures." So young John Fox Slater was hardly an impecunious youngster driven by hunger to establish his financial independence.

He attended academies in Plainfield, Connecticut, and in Wentham and Wilbraham, Massachusetts. At seventeen, he entered the family's business, a woolen mill, in Hopeville, Connecticut. He became manager of the mill when he was 21. This led to his managing another of his father's mills (this one, a cotton mill) in Jewett City, Connecticut.

In 1842 he removed to Norwich, Connecticut, where he made his home for the remainder of his life. In Norwich in 1844, he met and married Marianna Hubbard. The couple had six children. The year before his marriage, Slater inherited a modest fortune when his father died. At once, he and his brother, William S. Slater, formed a partnership to manufacture cotton and woolen goods. Their partnership flourished. When in 1871 they built the Ponemah mill at Taftville, Connecticut, it was said to be the largest plant of its kind in the world.

[2] William Adams Brown, *Morris Ketcham Jesup: A Character Sketch* (New York: Charles Scribner's Sons, 1910), p. 72.

The brother's partnership was dissolved in 1872. Thereafter John Fox Slater took an interest in railroad investments. Over half the endowment that Slater turned over to the Slater Fund trustees in 1882 was in railroad bonds.

Slater's choice of trustees was generally quite good. There were only two instances of non-performance among chosen trustees: W. E. Dodge, Sr., and Phillips Brooks. Dodge, the oldest trustee, ten years senior to Slater, the founder, died on February 9, 1883, after the second meeting of the trustees without having attended any board meetings owing to his having been in Europe and California respectively at the time of the first two meetings. At his death, he was replaced by his son on the Slater board. On the other hand, Brooks repeatedly made known his desire to resign from the board. He attended only one board meeting, and his resignation was finally accepted January 5, 1889.

Why were Dodge and Brooks chosen as trustees? Dodge was a friend of Slater and had a record of interest in support of schools for blacks. Both men had high visibility and doubtless added prestige to the fledgling fund in their roles as trustees. Although Dodge's age might be a deterent to his selection, he was a vigorous man almost to the date of his death. Slater consulted him regarding the establishment of his fund and the choice of trustees.

### William Earl Dodge, Sr.

W. E. Dodge, Sr., experienced a socially modest childhood which, with the help of hard work and good connections, developed into an opulent adulthood. Born in Hartford in 1805, Dodge received a common school education, then went to work at his father's cotton mill. At the age of thirteen, Dodge moved with his family to New York City where he went to work in a wholesale dry goods store, remaining for eight years. As a young man in his early twenties, he entered the wholesale dry goods business for himself. In 1833, he married Melissa, the daughter of Anson Phelps and thereupon became a member of the firm of Phelps, Dodge & Company, a firm which he headed until 1879.

As his fortune and influence swelled, he developed interests in railroads and insurance companies. He purchased vast areas of woodlands in Michigan, Pennsylvania, Georgia, and Canada. He developed lumber and mill interests, coal and iron mines, and copper mines near Lake Superior.

Dodge became a prestigious merchant. He was one of the first directors of the Erie Railroad. He was a director of the United States Trust Company, Western Union, and a number of other leading firms. He was elected president of the New York Chamber of Commerce three times in succession.

In an effort to head off the breakup of the Union and the losses that would accrue to New York creditors of southern firms, he became a delegate to the Peace Convention in Washington in February 1861. Once civil conflict came, he loyally supported the Union cause. After the war, he served a term in the United States House of Representatives beginning in 1867 when he represented the cause of protectionism for American industry. Later he served an appointment to the Indian Commission proferred by President Grant.

Along with his passion for business and public service, Dodge evidenced intense interest in the world of religion. A Congregationalist turned Presbyterian, Dodge was a staunch Sabbatarian and president of several temperance associations. He evinced an interest in his church's foreign missions and aided the freedmen. Several times he was a commissioner to the General Assembly of the Presbyterian Church, a trustee of Union Theological Seminary in New York, and vice president of the American Bible Society.

At one time, Dodge supported efforts to return blacks from America to Africa. But with the manumission of blacks and the responsibilities of citizenship conferred upon them, Dodge came to believe that education for the freedmen was of supreme importance. Accordingly, prior to the establishment of the Slater Fund, Dodge contributed to the support of schools for blacks, believing education to be the primary and most comprehensive need of the Negro. He contributed to Lincoln University in Oxford, Pennsylvania, Zion Wesley College, Hampton Institute, Howard University, Atlanta University, and Biddle University.

Following his death on February 9, 1883, the New York State Chamber of Commerce provided a bronze statue of Dodge which was erected at the juncture of Broadway and Sixth Avenue in New York City.

In this century, Dodge has not been forgotten. His life was the subject of a doctoral dissertation at Columbia University in 1951, a thesis which was published in book form.[3] Surely William Earl

[3] Richard Lowitt, *A Merchant Prince of the Nineteenth Century: William E. Dodge* (New York: Columbia University Press, 1952).

Dodge, Sr., was a sufficiently formidable personage to add luster to the Slater Fund and its purposes. Dodge was well enough regarded by his fellow trustees that, at his death, his son, William E. Dodge, Jr., was chosen to replace him.

## Phillips Brooks

The other non-performer among trustees chosen by Slater was Phillips Brooks, one of the best known and beloved American clerics of the time. His very name enhanced the prestige of the Slater trust even as he persistently chose not to serve. Despite his non-appearance at meetings of the board, his fellow trustees placed him on the executive committee when they met at their fifth session, October 2-3, 1884. Thereupon Brooks attended the next meeting of the board, a special session at the Fifth Avenue Hotel in New York City on January 17, 1885. But he never came back.

Brooks was born in Boston in 1835 of old New England stock in both his father's and mother's families. He was the second of six sons, four of whom entered the ministry. When he was born, his mother, Mary Ann Phillips, was a Unitarian. But she converted to the Episcopal Church a few years after his birth.

Brooks entered Harvard College in 1851. Upon graduation, he taught briefly and without satisfaction at Boston Latin School wherein he was once a student. Thereupon he was persuaded to enter the Virginia Theological Seminary in Alexandria. The school was a stronghold of the evangelical, low church, or methodist party in the Episcopal Church. Brooks was ordained deacon in 1859 and entered upon his duties as rector of the Church of the Advent in Philadelphia the same year.

In 1862, he became rector of Holy Trinity Church, Philadelphia, where he became identified with the Broad Church movement, which to him meant "a closer relation between God and man." He became the leading light of broad churchmanship in America for the balance of his career.

He travelled abroad in 1865, in Europe and the Holy Land. He managed to visit Europe every alternate summer for close to thirty years. In 1868 he wrote the Christmas hymn, "O Little Town of Bethlehem," an inspiration derived from his visit to Palestine three years earlier.

In 1869 he accepted the rectorship of Trinity Church, Boston, the largest and wealthiest Protestant Episcopal Church in the city. The edifice the church currently occupies was constructed under his direction. Brooks consistently packed the pews and popularized the Episcopal Church in the den of Puritanism and Unitarianism. As a homiletician, Brooks had few peers. In the pulpit he was a commanding figure, not alone for his size (he was six feet four in height, and his summital weight was 300 pounds), but for his intense, rapid-fire delivery and magnetic personality which drew to him people of varied persuasions. He was widely popular outside his own denomination. He knew how to convey deeply spiritual traditional Christianity in a practical way so that his audiences were enthralled and came back repeatedly for more.

When he was chosen by John F. Slater as a trustee, Brooks was rector of Trinity Church in Boston with his pulpit reputation already well established. In 1877 he had delivered a series, "Lectures on Preaching," at the Yale Divinity School. The series was published the same year.[4] In 1878 he published his first volume of sermons. And in 1879 at the Philadelphia Divinity School, he delivered the Bohlen Lectures (established 1875) on "The Influence of Jesus."

While he was a Slater trustee (1882-89), he published a volume, *Sermons Preached in English Churches* (1883), received an honorary degree of Doctor of Divinity from Oxford University (1885), and declined election as assistant bishop of the diocese of Pennsylvania (1886).

In the latter year, at the General Convention of the Protestant Episcopal Church, Brooks led the opposition to a resolution to change the name of the church to "The American Church" or "the Church of the United States." Either name would have been consonant with the name of the mother church, "The Church of England." But Brooks protested the presumption, as he saw it, of an assumption that apostolic succession conferred exclusive privileges.

Although the resolution did not pass, Brooks, seeing the possibility that the issue would be raised again at subsequent conventions, inveighed against the name change, or the idea which propelled it, after the 1886 convention ended. He sermonized that, if the change were made, "he did not see how he or any who did not believe in apostolic succession could remain in the Episcopal Church." Brooks' stand cost him in terms of support among high churchmen, but it had an important influence both in America and in England.

[4] In 1964, Seabury republished Brooks' *Lectures on Preaching* (first published in 1877) as Phillips Brooks, *On Preaching*.

In 1886 Brooks published another volume of sermons. The following year, Columbia University conferred an honorary DD. degree on him. In January 1889, his resignation as Slater trustee was accepted. During Lent, 1890, he followed the lead of Bishop Potter of New York and conducted a remarkable series of noontime services in Trinity Church in lower Manhattan, addressing overflow crowds of businessmen in what became an important personal triumph.

Brooks was elected Episcopal bishop of Massachusetts in 1891. Reflecting the party spirit that he had aroused, his election was challenged by those who attacked his alleged doctrinal unsoundness and eccelesiastical latitudinarianism. Finally, after ten weeks when the issue was in doubt, a majority of bishops confirmed his election, and he entered upon his episcopal duties. These he administered with perfect decorum despite his reputation for being largely indifferent to convention.

He was only 57 when he died, January 23, 1893. His death was treated as a public calamity on both sides of the Atlantic. In his memory, Phillips Brooks House was established at Harvard, and a bronze statue of him by Saint-Gaudens was erected in Copley Square, Boston. He was memorialized in Westminster Abbey, London.

Brooks possessed great humor and simplicity, his dress was unconventional, and he was much loved. He had a truly magnetic personality which never shone more brilliantly than when he was in the pulpit. His sermons continue to be reprinted, and a biography was published by MacMillan in 1961.[5] It is quite obvious why he was sought as a trustee of the Slater Fund.

## Rutherford Birchard Hayes

As to the most active trustees during the period 1882-1891, none was more prestigious than the president of the board, R. B. Hayes, former president of the United States. And none was more active in pursuing the purposes of the trust during his incumbency. Hayes attempted to retire to private life in 1874 when he became heir to his uncle Sardis Birchard's estate. But he was soon drawn back to public life, being re-elected governor of Ohio in 1875 and elected

[5] Raymond Wolfe Albright, *Focus on Infinity: A Life of Phillips Brooks* (New York: MacMillan, 1961).

president the following year. In his acceptance of the presidency, he limited himself to serving one term, following the extraordinarily successful example of President Polk.

At the conclusion of his presidential term in 1881, Hayes limited his activities to those of a reformer and philanthropist, no small part of which were devoted to his duties as president of the Slater board. Hayes was also president of the National Prison Association (1883-1893), having previously shown an interest in prison reform as governor of Ohio following his election in 1867. Hayes also served as trustee of Ohio State University (which was founded in 1870 when he was governor) and the Peabody Education Fund.

Hayes was one of a succession of presidents from Ohio who distinguished themselves in battle in the Civil War and thus qualified for political office. In 1861 Hayes was appointed Major of the 23rd Ohio Infantry, distinguished himself in several battles in the Virginia theater, was wounded four times, became judge-advocate, and was promoted to Major General. He was elected a member of congress from his Ohio district in 1864 without campaigning. In June 1865, he resigned his commission and took his seat in the House the following December. He was re-elected in 1866 for another term after which he ran for and was elected governor of Ohio. As governor, he championed merit in appointments, charitable and prison reform, care for the insane, and the completion of a state geological survey.

As president, Hayes ended Reconstruction by withdrawing troops from the last of the occupied southern states; he unsuccessfully proposed civil service reform, and strictly adhered to the gold standard. His successor in the White House, James A. Garfield, was Hayes' friend and political supporter.

Hayes was born to Rutherford and Sophia Birchard Hayes in Delaware, Ohio, in 1822. His forebears had lived in Windsor, Connecticut. Hayes' father died prior to the boy's birth. The primary masculine influence in Hayes' formative years was his mother's brother, Sardis Birchard.

Hayes attended academies at Norwalk, Ohio, and Middletown, Connecticut, after which he entered Kenyon College, an Episcopal church-related school in Gambier, Ohio, whence he graduated in 1842 at the head of his class. He next entered Harvard Law School, where he was a classmate of and shared lodgings with J. L. M. Curry, later a fellow trustee of both the Peabody and Slater funds.

Hayes was admitted to the Ohio bar in 1845 and began his practice in Lower Sandusky (later renamed Fremont), Ohio. In 1848 he spent the summer in Texas (for health reasons) with a college friend, Guy M. Bryan. In 1850 he removed to Cincinnati, Ohio's leading city at that time, where, after a brief period of meager practice, he flourished as a criminal lawyer.

In 1852 Hayes married Lucy Webb, daughter of James Webb, a Chillicothe, Ohio, physician. Rutherford and Lucy had seven sons and a daughter. Upon reaching the White House, Lucy was the first First Lady with a college education, having graduated from Cincinnati's Wesleyan Female College.

Hayes was a cut above the leading national political lights of his time both intellectually and in terms of affectional powers. He was never seduced by the self-serving hokum of acquisitive businessmen which justified a "public be damned" and "winner take all" attitude. Hayes did not forget his roots, and his experience as a criminal lawyer rather than, say, a corporate lawyer likely produced in him a particular attitude toward people which served him well as head of a foundation established to educationally help the most disadvantaged people in America, the freedmen.

Hayes never failed to attend a meeting of the Slater trustees during the period of this study (1882-91). Although the death of his wife, Lucy, in June 1889 was a greatly affecting loss to him, Hayes never faltered in attending to the interests of the trust. He died on January 17, 1893, after a brief interval of sickness and was succeeded by Daniel C. Gilman as president. During his tenure on the board, Hayes was a member of the executive committee beginning in 1882. When the education committee was formed in 1890, Hayes served as a member *ex officio*.

Hayes continues to have a hold on biographers and historians. His diary and/or correspondence have been edited and published no less than three times in different forms in the twentieth century.[6] In addition, a study of his speeches, a University of Michigan doctoral thesis, and a "Chronology, documents, and biographical aids" to his

[6] Louis D. Rubin, Jr. (ed.) *Teach the Freeman: The Correspondence of Rutherford B. Hayes and the Slater Fund for Negro Education* (Baton Rouge: Louisiana State University Press, 1959). 2 vols.

Charles Richard Williams (ed.) *Diary and Letters of Rutherford Birchard Hayes: Nineteenth President of the United States* (Columbus: The Ohio State Archeological and Historical Society, 1922-1926). 5 vols. Hereinafter cited as Williams, *Hayes' Diary and Letters.*

T. Harry Williams (ed.) *Hayes: The Diary of a President, 1875-81* (New York: David McKay Company, 1964).

life have been wrought.[7] All this and at least four biographies attest to the continuing fascination of the man for scholars.[8] Of course, it should be noted that his meticulously-kept diary and correspondence make him one of the most accessible national figures to write about.

## Morris Ketchum Jesup

Next to Hayes, the most influential trustee in the formative years of the Slater Fund was undoubtedly M. K. Jesup, a native of Westport, Connecticut, who moved to New York with his mother as a child. His parents were Charles (a Yale graduate who died in 1837 leaving his widow in financial straits) and Abigail Sherwood Jesup. During the relatively brief time he attended school in New York City, he was a friend and schoolmate of William E. Dodge, Jr., a fellow Slater trustee. Jesup was born in 1830, two years before Dodge's birth.

Jesup went to work at age twelve for the firm of Rogers, Ketchum, and Grosvenor, a firm which later became the Rogers Locomotive Works. At the age of 24, he was self-employed with a partner, handling railroad supplies in the firm of Clark & Jesup. In 1857, he formed M. K. Jesup & Company with another partner, John S. Kennedy. The firm dealt in railroad supplies, but drifted into doing a banking business. The Kennedy partnership was dissolved after ten years. In 1870, M. K. Jesup & Company became M. K. Jesup, Paton & Company with a new partner, John Paton. Jesup retired in 1884 at which time the firm's name became John Paton & Company. Following Paton's death, the firm became known as Cuyler, Morgan & Company of which Jesup remained a special partner.

Beginning in 1884, Jesup devoted himself to his philanthropies with the same zeal that he applied to business. His interest in good works, however, had been aroused prior to his retirement. In 1858,

[7] See Upton Sinclair Palmer, "An Historical and Critical Study of the Speeches of Rutherford B. Hayes" (Ann Arbor: University Microfilms, 1950); and Arthur Bishop (ed.) *R. B. Hayes, 1822-93, Chronology, Documents, Biographical Aids* (Dobbs Ferry, NY: Oceana Publications, 1969).

[8] See Harry Barnard, *Rutherford B. Hayes and His America* (New York: Russell & Russell, 1967); Kenneth E. Davison, *The Presidency of Rutherford B. Hayes* (Westport, CT: Greenwood Press, 1972); Hamilton James Eckenrode, *Rutherford B. Hayes: Statesman of Reunion* (Port Washington, NY: Kenikat Press, 1963): and Charles Richard Williams, *The Life of Rutherford Birchard Hayes, Nineteenth President of the United States* (New York: DaCapo Press, 1971). Reprint of volume published by Houghton Mifflin (Boston) in 1914.

while on a business trip to Richmond, Jesup witnessed a slave auction. His revulsion from the scene of inhumanity caused him to believe that the abolition of slavery should have primary priority. Thereafter he was a devoted friend of blacks.

Jesup served as president of New York's Five Points House of Industry in 1860. During the Civil War, he was one of the organizers of the United States Christian Commission, an interdenominational organization the purpose of which was to provide personal supplies, communication with loved ones at home, and uplifting comforts and diversions for soldiers.

In 1881 Jesup became president of his chief philanthropic interest, the American Museum of Natural History in New York City. Jesup gave a million dollars to the museum in his lifetime and an equal amount in his will. He wished the museum to be the best of its kind in the world.

Also in 1881, Jesup was president of the New York City Mission and Tract Society for which he built the DeWitt Memorial Chapel, an institutional church, named in memory of his father-in-law, Reverend Thomas DeWitt. Jesup was in the forefront of the most progressive and enlightened efforts to uplift the human condition.

In 1882 Jesup became trustee and treasurer of the John F. Slater Fund, in which work he was very active. Jesup also served as vice president of the Evangelical Alliance, a 19th century predecessor of the Federal and National Council of Churches of Christ in the United States. Likewise, he was a vice president of the Society for the Prevention of Cruelty to Animals, the Society for the Suppression of Vice, and the Institution for the Instruction of the Deaf and Dumb. He supported Anthony Comstock's efforts to suppress pornography.

Jesup's money aided a number of institutions of higher learning including Union Theological Seminary of New York (of which Jesup was a trustee), the Syrian Protestant College of Beirut, Hampton Institute, Tuskegee, Yale, Harvard, Williams, and Princeton. The Jesup Psychological Laboratory at George Peabody College for Teachers in Nashville was funded by and named for him. Jesup was prominently identified with the Metropolitan Museum of Art in New York City.

Jesup supported the Carl Lumholtz expedition (1890-97) to study the Indians of northern Mexico, and the Jesup North Pacific Expedition (1897) to study the migrations that occurred between Asia and North America. Jesup was president of the Audobon

Society (1897-1908). He also served as president of the Peary Arctic Club which was instrumental in supporting Peary's expedition to discover the North Pole. It is unfortunate that Jesup's death on January 22, 1908, prevented his knowing of Peary's discovery which came later the same year. Peary honored Jesup by naming the most northern point of Greenland, Cape Morris K. Jesup.

One of Jesup's last honors was to be named a member of the General Education Board when it was established in 1902. He was a trustee of the Brick Presbyterian Church in New York City and a member of numerous organizations, including the New York Yacht Club, the Sons of the American Revolution, and the Metropolitan Club of Washington. From 1899 to 1907, he served as president of the New York State Chamber of Commerce.

While Jesup could not possibly give unremitting time and attention to all the organizations with which he (or his name) was associated, it is clear that he had enormous reserves of energy and stamina. He did not permit his efforts to flag in carrying out his duties as Slater Fund treasurer while he had other philanthropic interests with demands upon his time and attention. He attended all but three of the first fifteen Slater board meetings and lent a strong sense of accountability to the operations of the fund while he served as Slater treasurer and member of the finance committee, positions he held from 1882 until his death in 1908. Beginning in 1891, Jesup was an *ex officio* member of the education committee.

His interests were broad and his name was one calculated to bring prestige to whatever cause to which he lent it. Although Jesup has been largely neglected by biographers, only one volume having been produced to render his memory timeless (and that only two years after his death),[9] Jesup was a good choice as Slater trustee.

## Daniel Coit Gilman

D. C. Gilman, a pioneer in the development of the modern American university, was the first secretary of the Slater board. He assumed the presidency of the board at Hayes' death in 1893 and remained president until his own death in 1908.

Gilman was a native of John Fox Slater's adopted home town, Norwich, Connecticut, where he was born in 1831 and where he delivered an historical discourse on September 7, 1859, on the

[9] William Adams Brown, *op. cit.*.

occasion of the bicentennial observance of the settlement of the town.[10]

Gilman was the son of William Charles (a prosperous businessman) and Eliza Coit Gilman. As a student, he had the great good fortune of coming into contact with a great number of students and teachers who attained distinction in academia. The relationships which he developed should have and apparently did develop an interest in young Gilman which boded well for his success as an educator of the first rank.

When he attended the Norwich Academy, one of his schoolmates was Timothy Dwight, grandson of a Yale president and himself president of Yale by 1886 when he transformed Yale from a small, parochial, albeit distinguished, college into a modern university of the first rank.

Gilman entered Yale College in 1848 when Theodore Dwight Woolsey, clergyman and political scientist, was president. Benjamin Silliman, Denison Olmsted, James Dwight Dana, and James Hadley were professors. Silliman was professor of chemistry and natural history at Yale from 1802 till 1853. He was the most prominent and influential scientific man in America during the first half of the nineteenth century. When Gilman was a student at Yale, Denison Olmsted was professor of natural philosophy and astronomy.

James Dwight Dana succeeded Silliman as professor of natural history at Yale in 1849. He was a master of geology, mineralogy, and zoology. He published the standard works of the time in geology and mineralogy. Gilman published his biography in 1899.[11]

James Hadley was appointed tutor at Yale in 1845 and became assistant professor of Greek in 1848, the year Gilman matriculated. Gilman became a close friend of Andrew Dickson White, a fellow student at Yale, who, armed with ideas framed in exposure to European universities, did for Cornell, a state university in New York, what Gilman later did for Johns Hopkins.

After graduating from Yale in 1852, Gilman attended Harvard and lived in a house he shared with Professor Arnold Guyot in Cambridge. A geographer, Guyot lectured for the Massachusetts Board of Education in institutes and normal schools. He nurtured Gilman's interest in geography.

[10] Gilman's address was published at Boston by G. C. Rand and Avery, city printers, 1859.

[11] D. C. Gilman, *The Life of James Dwight Dana, Scientific Explorer, Mineralogist, Geologist, Zoologist, Professor in Yale University* (New York: Harper & Brothers, 1899).

In 1853 Gilman sailed with A. D. White to Europe where each served as attache in the United States mission to the imperial court in Saint Petersburg. Gilman stayed two years, then returned to Yale for the next dozen years.

Gilman became professor of physical geography and college librarian and organized and headed the Sheffield Scientific School, Yale's school of science. In funding the school, Gilman used Morrill Act funds (authorized in 1862), the first instance of their use by any institution.

In 1861 Gilman married Mary Ketcham of New York City, who lived until 1869. In 1877 he married Elizabeth Dwight Woolsey, of the Yale family, who survived Gilman, succumbing in 1910.

From 1872 to 1875, Gilman served as the first president of the University of California in Berkeley where he initiated some of the educational innovations which he later brought to fruition at Johns Hopkins and where he was able to secure several notable gifts for the university.

From 1875 to 1901, Gilman served as the first president of the Johns Hopkins University in Baltimore. He recruited an outstanding faculty for the new school and placed emphasis upon graduate studies, academic freedom, and research. Despite the generous endowment in securities and land of the school and hospital by the founder, a Quaker citizen of Baltimore, the school's opening was not unattended by untoward reverses. The University was hurt when the Baltimore & Ohio Railroad suspended dividends on common stock (the bulk of Johns Hopkins' endowment) in 1876. The opening of the medical school was actually deferred until 1893.

Gilman became a Slater trustee in 1882 and remained so until his death in 1908. In 1883 Gilman published his life of President James Monroe.[12] He took leave of absence from Johns Hopkins in 1889-90 when he travelled in the Orient. He served as a Peabody Education Fund trustee beginning in 1893. In 1896-97 Gilman served along with his friend, A. D. White, and others as a member of the United States Commission to investigate and report upon the true divisional line between Venezuela and British Guiana.

Following his retirement as president of the Johns Hopkins, Gilman went to Washington as founding president of the Carnegie Institution, a research organization established by Andrew Carne-

[12] D. C. Gilman, *James Monroe* (Boston: Houghton Mifflin, 1883). The book was republished in 1970 by Arlington House, New Rochelle, NY. An 1898 edition of the biography was reprinted in 1972 by AMS Press, New York City.

gie in 1902. From this position, he resigned after only three years, feeling that he did not have as free a hand in administering the organization as he desired.

Also in 1902, Gilman became a member of the General Education Board, a foundation which aided education in the southern states with an original endowment of $130 million. From 1901 to 1907, Gilman was president of the National Civil Service Reform League. Gilman's interest in the federal civil service accompanied his manifest interest in history and political science.

In 1907, the year before his death, Gilman became a trustee of the Russell Sage Foundation, an institution established with an original endowment of $10 million the aim of which was to remove the causes of poverty so that the poor might be able to earn enough to provide sanitary homes, nutritious food, and the blessings of good health for themselves and their children.

Gilman has had two biographers since his death, the first being Abraham Flexner, the authority on higher education, particularly medical education. Flexner studied at Hopkins when Gilman was president. He regarded Gilman as having created an American style of university. Gilman's second biographer is Francesco Cordasco who credits Gilman with shaping the Ph. D. degree to fit a variety of uses and ends.[13]

Gilman's impact upon higher education, especially graduate, research, and medical, is well documented. His 1898 volume, *University Problems in the United States,* reflecting his views of what the American university should be, continues to be reprinted and read.[14] His choice as a Slater trustee provided the fund with both prestige and expert educational counsel.

### Morrison Remick Waite

Morrison R. Waite, Chief Justice of the United States, was, next to William E. Dodge, Sr., the oldest trustee selected by Slater. Waite,

[13] See Abraham Flexner, *Daniel Coit Gilman, Creator of the American Type of University* (New York: Harcourt, Brace & Company, 1946); and Francesco Cordasco, *Daniel Coit Gilman and the Protean Ph.D.; The Shaping of American Graduate Education* Leiden: E. J. Brill, 1960). Cordasco's biography was reprinted in 1973 by Rowman & Littlefield of Totowa, NJ. under the title: *The Shaping of American Graduate Education: Daniel Coit Gilman and the Protean Ph.D.*.

[14] See Daniel C. Gilman, *University Problems in the United States* (New York: The Century Company, 1898), reprinted by the Garrett Press and the Arno Press (both NY.) in 1969, and by the Johnson Reprint Corporation (NY.) in 1971.

born in 1816, was only a year younger than Slater. He was the board's first vice president and a member of the executive committee beginning in 1883. The faithfulness of the board's president (Hayes) in attending the board's meetings scarcely gave Waite the opportunity to actively chair meetings or give personal direction to the deliberations or operations of the board. Waite attended five of the nine meetings of the board which were held prior to his death on March 23, 1888. Waite was not unfamiliar with the ways of educational trustees. He had served as a Peabody Education Fund trustee from 1874 and as a member of the Yale Corporation, the university's governing body, concurrently with his Slater connection.

Waite was the son of Henry Matson and Maria Selden Waite. His father served as Chief Justice of the Connecticut Supreme Court from 1854 to 1857. The younger Waite graduated from Yale in 1837 as did William E. Evarts and Samuel J. Tilden, lawyers who were active in destroying the infamous Tweed ring in New York City.

Beginning in 1838, Waite practiced law with Samuel M. Young in Maumee City, Ohio. The firm moved to Toledo in 1850. Waite's legal practice dealt with financial adjustments, mortgage foreclosures, and titles. By 1851 Waite had become one of the recognized leaders of the Ohio bar.

Prior to aligning with the new Republican Party in 1860, Waite had been a Whig, supporting Harrison for president in 1840. During the Civil War, he was a strong unionist. But it was not until Grant's administration that Waite began to receive national recognition. In 1871 President Grant appointed him American counsel in the Geneva arbitration of the *Alabama* Claims between the United States and Great Britain. The dispute dealt with claimed indemnities for the use of British ports by Confederate cruisers. In the arbitration, Waite served alongside his old Yale classmate, William Evarts, and Caleb Cushing, whose international credentials included the successful leadership of an American delegation which in 1844 signed a convention with the imperial minister in Peking which secured commercial privileges for Americans in China's open ports.

In 1873, Waite was elected president of Ohio's constitutional convention. But it was his arbitration work in Geneva that subsequently led to his appointment as Chief Justice of the United States by President Grant in 1874 upon the death of Salmon P. Chase, another Chief Justice from Ohio. Waite's nomination was confirmed by the Senate without dissent.

The Waite court (1874-88) was called upon to decide a number of momentous cases involving the Civil War constitutional amendments, states rights, and the development of states and territories in the West, including the construction of transcontinental railroads, the rise of agrarianism, control of public utilities and their rates. Other questions that appeared on the Waite court's agenda arose out of industrial strikes, anarchist riots, polygamy, anti-Chinese legislation, state and municipal debt repudiation, and the constitutionality of Reconstruction acts. Waite's biographer, Bruce Raymond Trimble, believed that Waite, as Chief Justice, worked hard to defend the public's interests.

Following his elevation to the U. S. Supreme Court in 1874, Waite became a trustee of the Peabody Education Fund in the affairs of which he became absorbed. In 1880, Waite helped revise a Peabody Fund report titled, "Education for the Colored Population of the United States." The report was a strong appeal to Congress to favorably consider aiding black education with federal funds. Waite signed the report, a report which answered criticisms that federal aid to education was unconstitutional. The report was issued in support of the Blair Bill, sponsored by New Hampshire Senator Henry W. Blair. Thus Waite, while Chief Justice, lobbied in behalf of a bill before Congress and gave an ex parte opinion that the bill was constitutional.

When Rutherford Hayes came to Washington as president, he and Chief Justice Waite became close friends. In 1882, when John Fox Slater was in the process of getting the Slater Fund established, Waite used his influence to get Hayes, his friend and fellow Peabody trustee, to accept the presidency of the trust. Waite agreed to serve as vice president.

Waite has had two biographers in the twentieth century, both of whom give him high marks as a jurist.[15] Since 1959, the Library of Congress has held Waite's papers containing approximately 20,000 items, a gift of the Chief Justice's grandson, M. R. Waite, of Cincinnati.

## Melville Weston Fuller

Waite was succeeded on the Slater board by the man who succeeded him on the Supreme Court, M. W. Fuller. Born in 1833 in

[15] See Peter C. Magrath, *Morrison R. Waite: The Triumph of Character* (New York: MacMillan, 1963); and Bruce Raymond Trimble, *Chief Justice Waite: Defender of the Public Interest* (Princeton: Princeton University Press, 1938).

Augusta, Maine, to Frederick Augustus (a lawyer) and Catherine Martin Weston Fuller, Fuller graduated from Bowdoin College in 1853, was elected to Phi Beta Kappa, then attended Harvard law school, read law, was admitted to the Maine bar in 1855, and began the practice of law in Augusta.

The following year, Fuller moved to Chicago where his reputation was made in the law. He became prominent in cases involving the public interest as in litigation over control of the Chicago lake front (The City of Chicago versus the Illinois Central Railroad), his fight against monopolistic contracts controlled by gas companies in Chicago, and monopolistic franchises given to street railways by the State of Illinois.

Fuller was a leading layman of the Protestant Episcopal Church, a vestryman and lay reader in Saint Mark's Church in Chicago, and a delegate to several triennial General Conventions of the church. And his legal reputation rested partially upon his defense of Charles Edward Cheney, rector of Christ Church (Episcopal) in Chicago in a celebrated heresy trial and subsequent case that went before the Illinois Supreme Court involving efforts to prohibit Cheney from using Christ Church and its rectory. The cases were issues leading to the establishment of the Reformed Episcopal Church in December 1873 into which Cheney's congregation followed him and in which he became a bishop.

Fuller was a lifetime Democrat who believed in states' rights and individualism. He was no reformer, believing in traditional rights of property and freedom of contract. When President Grover Cleveland nominated him to succeed Waite as Chief Justice in 1888, there was strong partisan opposition to him which delayed his confirmation by the Senate. His nomination at length was approved by a vote of 41 to 20.

Fuller was a regent of the Smithsonian Institution of Washington and a trustee of both the Peabody and Slater funds beginning in 1888. Fuller began serving as a vice president of the Slater board in 1891. He became a trustee of Bowdoin College, his alma mater, in 1894. He became a member of the Permanent Court of Arbitration at the Hague in 1900. The following year, he was elected chairman of the Peabody Education Fund. Fuller also served as Executive Councillor of the American Society of International Law and was elected a Fellow of the American Academy of Arts and Sciences of Boston. He was awarded honorary LL.D. degrees by Bowdoin (1888), Northwestern University (1888), Harvard (1891), Yale and

Dartmouth (1901). Fuller died in Sorrento, Maine, July 4, 1910. He has been the subject of a biography by Willard Leroy King published in 1967.[16] Fuller's and Waite's court records with respect to the rights of blacks are examined in chapter nine.

**William Albert Slater**

The son of the founder, William A. Slater, was only 25 years of age when he was selected to be a trustee by his father. He was by far the youngest trustee, but merited his father's confidence in him by faithful attendance upon board meetings. Of the first fifteen board meetings held (1882-1891), he attended twelve. In 1909, he was elected president of the board and served until two years before his death when ill health required him to curtail his activities.

When the Slater Fund was established, young William Slater was fresh out of Harvard, having received a B.A. degree in 1881. His life is largely the story of a man with financial advantages who made the most of what he fell heir to, living the life of an enlightened philanthropist and indulging his interests in leisure-time activities as befitted his station in life.

In 1885, he married Ellen Peck of Norwich, Connecticut, with whom he had two children. In November 1886, he transferred to the Free Academy of Norwich a building costing $160,000 which he had erected in memory of his father. The building was named Slater Memorial Hall. Later he added an art collection at an additional cost of $80,000.

He gave large contributions to charities and public institutions, including $375,000 to establish Backus Hospital and $15,000 to the YMCA, both in Norwich. At his death in 1919, he left bequests to the Norwich Free Academy, Backus Hospital, and the Slater Library in Jewett City, Connecticut, which he had built, equipped, and supported in life.

Slater was a yachtsman and possessed a large collection of paintings of great value. In 1905 he collaborated with Arthur Mahler and Carlos Blacker in producing the volume, *Paintings of the Louvre, Italian and Spanish.*[17] He also had interests in literature and

[16] Willard Leroy King, *Melville Weston Fuller, Chief Justice of the United States, 1888-1910* (New York: MacMillan, 1950). Reprinted in 1963 by University of Chicago Press.

[17] Arthur Mahler, Carlos Blacker and W. A. Slater, *Paintings of the Louvre, Italian and Spanish* (New York: Doubleday, Page & Company, 1905).

religion. He was widely regarded as a splendid man, a brilliant conversationalist, gentle yet strong, thoughtful and considerate of others. In his later years, he uncomplainedly endured pain.

He was a member of the Cosmos, Metropolitan, University, and Chevy Chase clubs in Washington where he died February 25, 1919. As a Slater trustee and heir of his father, he upheld the family's name and purposes of his father's philanthropies as well as anyone might.

### John Aikman Stewart

The longest lived of the original Slater trustees was John A. Stewart, who lived to the age of 104. Of the original trustees, only Dodge (born in 1805) and Chief Justice Waite (born in 1816) were senior to Stewart and Hayes, both of whom were born in 1822. Stewart lived until 1926, surviving all the other original trustees by at least seven years. William A. Slater lived until 1919, but he was Stewart's junior by 35 years.

Stewart was one of the most active trustees in the formative years, serving on the powerful finance committee and attending all but two of the first fifteen meetings of the trustees in the period 1882-1891. Stewart remained a Slater trustee until his death, remaining healthy and vigorous to the end.

Stewart was born in New York City of John, a native of the island of Lewis in the Hebrides, and Mary Aikman Stewart, a native of New York. He completed Columbia College in New York in 1840. After graduation, he became a civil engineer and helped to survey the line of the New York, Lake Erie and Western Railroad during 1840-42. He became clerk of the New York City board of education in 1842. Beginning in 1850, he was actuary of the United States Life Insurance Company.

In 1853, Stewart organized the United States Trust Company in New York City, of which the principal stockholders were John Jacob Astor, Royal Phelps, and Peter Cooper. W. E. Dodge, Sr., was a director of the firm. Stewart served as secretary of the firm until 1864 when he was elected president. In 1902 Stewart became chairman of the board, continuing in the position until his death in 1926.

Stewart was personally acquainted with all United States presidents from Abraham Lincoln to Calvin Coolidge. Briefly he served as Assistant Treasurer of the United States by appointment of President Lincoln, 1864-65.

His philanthropic interests led him to become a promoter of the American Bible Society and a trustee of the College of New Jersey (later Princeton University) from 1868 until his death. He also served as president *pro tempore* of Princeton, 1910–1912. His position as chief executive officer of a leading financial institution made him of substantial value to the Slater trust, particularly in view of his loyalty to the fund's interests.

**William Earl Dodge, Jr.**

The younger W. E. Dodge was, like his fellow trustee, W. A. Slater, the son of a wealthy man who was involved in the business world but was far more active in pursuing philanthropic and personal interests befitting the well-born. He was born in 1832 of the union of the junior member of Phelps, Dodge & Company and Melissa Phelps, a union which helped to bind the two families both socially and commercially. Young W. E. Dodge became a partner in the family business in 1864 and was identified with the family's mining, railroad, and religious interests.

Dodge was a founder and president of the New York City YMCA, vice president of the American Sunday School Union, chairman of the National Arbitration Committee, and trustee of the Carnegie Institution of Washington, of which his fellow Slater trustee, D. C. Gilman, was the first president.

He contributed handsomely to the New York Botanical and Zoological Gardens and was a leader, serving as president, of the Evangelical Alliance, an early attempt at church cooperation of which Dodge's fellow Slater trustee, Morris Jesup, served as vice president. The Alliance was formed in London in 1846 and brought to America in 1867. By 1900, its influence had waned. In 1908 it was replaced by the Federal Council of Churches of Christ in America.

Dodge was one of the most faithful of the Slater trustees in terms of attendance at meetings. He served alongside his boyhood friend and schoolmate, Morris Jesup, on the finance committee of the Slater board. He died at Bar Harbor, Maine, August 9, 1903.

**Henry Codman Potter**

On January 5, 1889, at the eleventh meeting of the Slater board, Henry C. Potter, Episcopal bishop of New York, was elected to fill the vacancy occasioned by the resignation of Phillips Brooks. Potter was an evangelical and early exponent of the social gospel as it applied to problems of the city, poverty, tenements, children in the slums, labor relations, the institutional church, and the church's duty to render social service.

Potter's family had a history of providing leadership to the church. Born in Schenectady to Alonzo and Sara Maria Nott Potter in 1835, he was the son and nephew of bishops. His early education was in Philadelphia after which he became an employee in a dry goods store. In August 1854, he underwent a religious experience, whereupon he enrolled in the Virginia Theological Seminary in Alexandria, the alma mater of his predecessor on the Slater board, Brooks, whence Potter graduated in 1857, two years prior to Brooks' graduation. The same year he married Eliza Rogers Jacobs of Lancaster county, Pennsylvania, and undertook parish work at Greenburg, Pennsylvania.

In 1859 he went as rector to Saint John's Church in Troy, New York. Here he became active in support of the YMCA. In April 1866, he reported to Trinity Church, Boston, as assistant rector. He assisted Manton Eastburn at Trinity; Eastburn later became Episcopal bishop of Massachusetts. In 1869 Eastburn was succeeded at Trinity by Phillips Brooks who, in his turn, also became bishop of Massachusetts.

The year he went to Trinity in Boston, Potter became secretary to the House of Bishops. Moving on, Potter became rector of Grace Church, New York City, in 1868. Under his leadership, Grace Church became an activist church, that is, active in ministering to the whole man.

In 1883 Potter became bishop coadjutor of New York at the design of his uncle, Bishop Horatio Potter, who virtually retired and left the management of the diocese to his nephew. As an evangelical and broad churchman, H. C. Potter left his strong imprint on the affairs of the diocese through the next quarter of a century.

During the period 1884 to 1899, Potter helped to conciliate parties within the diocese which saw liberals pitted against conservatives, evangelicals against Anglo Catholics, and exponents of the "higher criticism" against biblical literalists. In one such case, Richard Heber Newton, rector of All Souls Church in New York City (1869–1902), held liberal views of the higher criticism. Both in 1884 and 1891, Potter refused to try Newton for heresy when presentments were made for the same. In 1902, Newton left for Palo Alto, California, as resident preacher at Stanford University.

In another case, Charles A. Briggs of the faculty of Union Theological Seminary in New York City had been convicted of heresy by the Presbyterians. When Briggs subsequently sought orders and was ordained by Potter, May 14, 1899, a storm was raised in the church by conservatives. Potter was vindicated, however, by Briggs' distinguished record as church presbyter following his ordination.

Potter inaugurated the precedent-setting Advent mission (an Episcopal church revival) in New York City in 1885. He also inaugurated retreats for the clergy and appealed for the erection of a cathedral (1887), which resulted in the beginnings of the Cathedral of Saint John the Divine in 1892. He early preached on the perils of wealth, indifference to social needs, and the duties of citizenship. He became a labor arbiter and social critic, publicly urging the end to police protection of vice in New York City in 1899.

Potter published *The Scholar and the State* in 1897, a book dealing with social ethics, learning, and scholarship which has been reprinted.[18] In 1902 he published *The Citizen in his Relation to the Industrial Situation;* and the following year, *The Modern Man and His Fellow Man.* Three biographies of Potter were published within 25 years of his death.[19]

As a distinguished churchman and one of the best known clergymen of his time, Potter lent the sort of welcome prestige to the Slater Fund that the founder and his successor fund managers sought in trustee appointments. Potter, however, like his predecessor, Phillips Brooks, represented a church which provided only moderate support to black people in America at a time when there were relatively few blacks living in major northern cities, the stronghold of the Episcopal Church.

Blacks came north in great numbers initially during World War I, several years after Potter's and Brooks' death. While Potter and other Episcopal Church leaders were among the first to become active in aiding demoralized denizens of the slums of northern cities, they were conspicuously less involved in helping blacks in the South to become self-sufficient (those the Slater fund primarily

[18] Henry Codman Potter, *The Scholar and the State, and Other Orations and Addresses* (New York: The Century Company, 1897). Reprinted in 1972 by Books for Libraries Press, Freeport, NY.

[19] See George Hodges, *Henry Codman Potter: Seventh Bishop of New York* (New York: Macmillan, 1915); Harriett A. Keyser, *Bishop Potter, the People's Friend* (New York, 1910); and James Sheerin, *Henry Codman Potter: An American Metropolitan* (New York: Fleming H. Revell, 1933).

sought to aid) than were Baptists, Congregationalists, Methodists, and Presbyterians. Among the latter, there was a strong abolitionist tradition which survived the Civil War and expressed itself in various measures aimed at aiding the freedman. There was no such tradition in most American churches, not alone the Episcopal Church. The lack thereof, however, did not deter Potter from rendering faithful service to the purposes of the Slater Fund until his death in 1908.

## James Petigru Boyce

Of the original ten Slater trustees, only two were from the South. One was a Baptist minister and educator, James P. Boyce, a native of South Carolina and founding president of the Southern Baptist Theological Seminary. Boyce was born in Charleston in 1827 to Ker (a Charleston cotton merchant and member of the South Carolina Senate) and Amanda Jane Caroline Johnston Boyce.

Boyce's collegiate education was secured at Charleston College and Brown University. He graduated from Brown in 1847, then enrolled in Princeton Seminary whence he graduated in 1851. The same year, he became a pastor in Columbia, South Carolina, then professor of theology at Furman University in Greenville in 1855.

He married Lizzie Llewellyn Ficklen in 1858. During his Greenville years, he had income from a farm as well as from his father. He became the first president of the Southern Baptist Theological Seminary in Greenville in 1859. The seminary was moved to Louisville, Kentucky, in 1877. Boyce served as president of the Southern Baptist Convention from 1872 to 1879.

Boyce held conservative theological opinions and published several volumes of sermons and theology beginning in 1856 and ending the year before his death. He found recreation in music, art, and poetry. He was highly prized as an executive and money raiser. He was a director of the Louisville Banking Company, the South Carolina Railroad Company, and the Graniteville Manufacturing Company (near Aiken, South Carolina).

The year before he died, Brown University awarded him an honorary LL.D. degree. Ill health led him to California, Alaska, and Europe in search of relief. He died in Pau, France, December 28, 1888. Despite his poor health toward the end, Boyce attended nine of the ten meetings of the Slater trustees held while he was a member of the board. He served as a member of the board's executive committee.

## John Albert Broadus

Boyce's successor both as president of the Southern Baptist Theological Seminary and as Slater trustee was a native Virginian, John Albert Broadus, who had been a close friend and coworker of Boyce at the seminary since its inception. Broadus and Boyce were the same age, and Broadus acknowledged that he never felt that he was quite the same after Boyce's death. "The old bouyancy never quite returned," He said.[20]

Broadus was the son of Edmond and Nancy Mims Broadus of Culpepper county, Virginia. From 1847 to 1850, he was a student at the University of Virginia, then pastor of the Baptist church in Charlottesville, university chaplain, and assistant instructor of ancient languages at the University. When the Southern Baptist Theological Seminary opened in Greenville, South Carolina, in 1859, Broadus occupied the Chair of New Testament and Homiletics.

During the Civil War, Broadus preached to the troops, served as corresponding secretary of the Southern Baptist Sunday School Board (of which, he was a cofounder), and during 1864-65 was aide-de-camp to Governor McGrath of South Carolina. Following the war, Broadus was back at the seminary despite its prostrate condition and gained a widespread reputation north and south as a preacher. In July 1870, he sailed for Europe for a year to recover his health. In 1877 the seminary moved to Louisville where additional funds and students assured its continuance.

Broadus was a member of the International Lesson Committee from 1878 to 1895. He delivered the Lyman Beecher Lectures at Yale in 1889, the same year he succeeded Boyce as president of the seminary and Slater trustee. He was greatly admired and loved and had a winning platform manner. From 1870 to 1893, a stream of books flowed from his pen beginning with *On the Preparation and Delivery of Sermons.*[21] In 1890, he published *Jesus of Nazareth.*[22] Both of these volumes have been republished in the late twentieth century.

Broadus died March 16, 1895, in Louisville, but he is still remembered as a master of homiletics. In 1956, Paul Huber wrote a

[20] Archibald Thomas Robertson, *Life and Letters of John Albert Broadus* (Philadelphia: American Baptist Publication Society, 1901), p. 374.

[21] See John A. Broadus, *On the Preparation and Delivery of Sermons,* rev. Vernon L. Stanfield (4th ed.; San Francisco: Harper & Row, 1979).

[22] See John A. Broadus, *Jesus of Nazareth* (Grand Rapids: Baker Book House, 1962).

doctoral thesis at the University of Michigan on the rhetorical theories of Broadus, and in 1959 an anthology of his sermons was published.[23] Archibald Thomas Robertson of the seminary faculty published a memorial volume of Broadus' life and letters.[24]

## Alfred Holt Colquitt

When John Fox Slater chose A. H. Colquitt as one of the original Slater trustees on March 4, 1882, Colquitt was serving as Governor of Georgia. Later that year he was elected to the United States Senate by the state legislature where he stayed until his death in 1894. Colquitt had previously served as a member of the United States Congress (1853-55), as a Major General in the Confederate States Army, and president of the Democratic State Convention in Georgia (1870).

Born in Walton county, Georgia, in 1824 to Walter T. (a United States Senator) and Nancy Lane Colquitt, A. H. Colquitt was graduated from the College of New Jersey in his twentieth year, admitted to the bar in 1845, and served in the Mexican War. He was married to Dorothy Tarver in 1848. At this period of his life, Colquitt lived on a plantation which his wife inherited in Baker county. Following his wife's death, Colquitt married Sarah Tarver, widow of Colquitt's brother-in-law.

Colquitt was regarded as a brilliant orator with an instinctive knowledge of the public pulse. Politically he was aligned with Henry W. Grady, the Atlanta editor, and other "New South" Democrats who sought industrial development of the region as a way out of its oppressive poverty. Religiously he was an active Methodist, licensed lay preacher, and a trustee of Emory College, the school Atticus Haygood, the Slater agent, served as president. Colquitt was elected president of the International Sunday School Convention in 1878.

His political enemies in Georgia accused him in 1880 of a corrupt bargain when he, as governor, appointed ex-governor Joseph E. Brown to fill the unexpired term of U. S. Senator John B. Gordon when the latter suddenly resigned. It was alleged that Gordon resigned in return for a promise of the presidency of the state-owned Western & Atlantic Railroad, then under Brown's

[23] See Paul Huber, "A Study of the Rhetorical Theories of John A. Broadus," (Ann Arbor: University Microfilms, 1956); and Vernon Latrelle Stanfield (ed.) *Favorite Sermons of John A. Broadus* (New York: Harper, 1959).

[24] See Archibald Thomas Robertson, *Op. cit.*.

control. In return for his appointment of Brown to the senate, Colquitt, it was further alleged, held a claim to Brown's political support. The charges, however, were unsubstantiated by convincing evidence and were not widely believed beyond the immediate circle of Colquitt's, Brown's, and Gordon's principal political detractors.

When Slater appointed Colquitt as a trustee, Colquitt possessed the attributes most admired by southerners in their elected officials, the moral triumvirate, "breeding, bravery, and piety,"[25] plus, of course, political influence deriving from holding public office and being an acknowledged master of platform presence. He had no background in philanthropy or the particular work the Slater trust was to undertake. But he was not alone in this shortcoming. He proved to be a dedicated trustee, serving on the executive committee and attending ten of the first fifteen meetings of the board in the period from inception to 1891. He was a person of influence and served the trust competently until his death on March 26, 1894.

## Jabez Lamar Monroe Curry

When J. L. M. Curry was appointed a Slater trustee in 1891 to assume the duties then relinquished by agent Haygood, he already had a reputation in educational foundation work as agent of the Peabody Education Fund dating from 1881. But he had a great deal more than that to commend him. He was recognized as a statesman, author, and educator.

Born in Lincoln county, Georgia, of William and Susan Winn Curry, J. L. M. Curry became a student at Waddell Academy in South Carolina, of which John C. Calhoun was a graduate. Curry entered Franklin College (later the University of Georgia) in 1839 and followed that educational experience with the study of law at Harvard which he entered in 1843. In Cambridge, he was a classmate of and shared lodgings in Mrs. Ford's boarding house with R. B. Hayes. While at Harvard, Curry heard Horace Mann, "father of the common schools," and was thereby influenced to favor universal education.

Since 1838 Curry had made his home in Talladega county, Alabama, where he practiced law prior to entering politics. In 1857

[25] Expression used in Gerald W. Johnson, *American Heroes and Hero Worship* (New York: Harper & Brothers, 1943). pp. 164-166.

he served as U. S. Congressman from Alabama until secession in 1861 when he left the Union with his state. He was a member of the Confederate States Congress in 1861-63 and 1864. During 1864 and 1865, he served on the staffs of General Joseph Eggleston Johnston, commander of the Army of Tennessee, and Major General Joseph Wheeler, chief of cavalry under Johnston.

Following the end of hostilities, Curry became president of impoverished Howard College, a Baptist-related school in Marion, Alabama, in 1865. In 1868 he became professor of English at Richmond College, now the University of Richmond, another Baptist-affiliated school. He declined a cabinet post tendered by his friend, Rutherford Hayes, in 1877. In 1881 he undertook the duties of the Peabody Fund agency. His tenure with the Peabody Fund was interrupted twice, first by his appointment as United States Minister to Spain (1885-88) and second as U. S. Ambassador Extraordinary to Spain in 1902.

In 1891 he combined his Peabody agency with the chairmanship of the education committee of the Slater Fund. At its founding in 1901, he became director of the Southern Education Board. During the period 1889-1901, Curry published several works of history, government, and biography. He has been the subject of biographies by Edwin Anderson Alderman and Armistead Churchill Gordon (co-authors) in 1911 and Jessie Pearl Rice in 1949.[26]

Curry was an ideal choice to succeed Haygood as the receptor and mediating agent of the Slater trustees in 1891 because of his experience as Peabody agent, the contacts he had cultivated in all sections of the country, and his enviable reputation as distinguished statesman, educator, and author. He commanded instant recognition wherever he went, and his dedication to the work at hand was manifest. Curry died in 1903.

## Atticus Greene Haygood

The first agent of the Slater trustees was the man who had provided the spark which caused John Fox Slater to establish his fund to aid black education. The spark was his book, *Our Brother in Black: His Freedom and His Future,* published in 1881.[27]

[26] Edwin Anderson Alderman and Armistead Churchill Gordon, *J. L. M. Curry: A Biography* (New York: MacMillan, 1911); and Jessie Pearl Rice, *J. L. M. Curry: Southerner, Statesman, and Educator* (New York: King's Crown Press, 1949).

[27] See Atticus G. Haygood, *Our Brother in Black: His Freedom and His Future* (Freeport, NY: Books for Libraries Press, 1970).

Haygood was born in Watkinsville, Georgia, in 1839 to Greene B., a lawyer from Clarke county, Georgia, and Martha Ann Askew Haygood, a teacher from North Carolina. A. G. Haygood was the oldest of eight children. His sister, Laura Askew Haygood, became noted as a missionary in China.

The Haygood family moved to Atlanta in 1852. His mother prepared young Atticus for entry into Emory College in Oxford in 1856 whence he graduated in 1859, the same year he married Mary Fletcher Yarborough of Oxford, and the year he was admitted on trial to the Georgia Conference of the Methodist Episcopal Church, South.

Early in 1861, Haygood was a unionist until Georgia seceded. Thereupon he became a secessionist and a sometime chaplain in the Confederate army. During most of the war, however, Haygood served as pastor of churches in the vicinity of Atlanta.

In 1870 Haygood was elected Sunday School Secretary of his church. His incumbency caused him to remove to Nashville, Tennessee. He published a missions tract, *Go or Send,* in 1874. The following year, he was elected president of his alma mater, Emory College, a position which he accepted and held for ten years.

He found Emory to be in debt, a condition common to virtually all schools in the late Confederate states. He provided intellectual vigor and administrative leadership which set the school's course toward more serious and pragmatic purposes and a more serious scholarly and vocational intensity on the part of the students.

For four years (1878-82), his collegiate responsibilities were shared with his editorial oversight of a new church periodical, the *Wesleyan Christian Advocate,* an organ of the Georgia and Florida conferences. He sharpened his journalistic skills as editor. His editorials paralleled those of the Atlanta *Constitution* in their approach toward "a New South."

Following his publication of *Our Brother in Black* in 1881, he was much in demand as a public speaker, primarily in the North. He became general agent of the Slater Fund the following year, a position he held jointly with his presidency of Emory College until December 1885 at which time, at the request of the Slater trustees, he relinquished the latter position. In 1883 he published a collection of *Sermons and Speeches* and in 1889 published two books, an edition of his speeches made as Slater agent titled, *Pleas for Progress,* and a study of the life of Jesus, *The Man of Galilee.*

In 1890 Haygood was elected bishop by the General Conference of his church meeting in St. Louis. He previously had been elected to the position in 1882, when he had been seeking the Slater position, but had declined. In 1890 he accepted and terminated his connection with the Slater Fund in May 1891. He immediately moved to Los Angeles, California, to assume his episcopal duties amidst two California and two Mexican conferences. His last years were an affliction of ill health and financial indebtedness, the latter due to his assumption of student and Emory College debts. His wife's health forced the family's return to Georgia in 1893. Haygood continued writing, producing a theological tome, *Jack-Knife and Brambles,* in 1893 and a novel about the Florentine monk, Savonarola, and the prince, Lorenzo de Medici, titled, *The Monk and the Prince,* in 1895. His articles appeared in *Harper's Magazine, Forum,* New York *Independent,* and *North American Review.*

Haygood's health failed rapidly in 1895, and he suffered three strokes of paralysis before his death on January 21, 1896. To the Slater Fund, as well as to everything else that he undertook, Haygood brought energy, enthusiasm, and clear thinking. His platform prowess and ability to write strong English were invaluable assets to his Slater work. In the twentieth century, Haygood has been the subject of a number of scholarly theses[28] and a full-length biography.[29]

[28] See, in particular, Marion L. Smith, "Atticus Greene Haygood: Christian Educator" (Unpublished Ph.D. Dissertation: Yale University, 1929).

[29] Harold W. Mann, *Atticus Greene Haygood: Methodist Bishop, Editor and Educator* (Athens: University of Georgia Press, 1965). Hereinafter cited as Mann, *Haygood.*

# Chapter 3

# Learning the Ropes

As directed by the trustees, Haygood's first task as general agent was to investigate the condition of Negro education in the southern states and report his findings, together with a plan of operations, to the Slater board.[1] This required that he travel throughout the South visiting schools for blacks and corresponding with school officials. He related that he was besieged with letters from individuals asking help for themselves or aid for their schools. He felt a need for secretarial assistance and wrote to Hayes that he had not only to answer inquiries but to distribute circulars to explain the aims and program of the foundation. He asked for $400 a year for secretarial assistance.[2]

In February 1883 Haygood went to Washington to address a meeting of educators on the Blair Bill for federal aid to education. The same month, the United States Congress passed a vote of thanks to John F. Slater for his gift to Negro education and requested the President to present him with a gold medal in the name of the people.[3]

The Slater Board met April 25 and 26, 1883, at the Fifth Avenue Hotel in New York City, all trustees being in attendance except for Waite and Brooks. After memorializing William E. Dodge, Sr., the trustee who died February 3, 1883, the trustees elected William E. Dodge, Jr., of New York to fill the vacancy.

The trustees established the fiscal year of the fund to begin September 1 of each year and specified that all annual reports from recipients would be prepared on the basis of the fiscal year. They received a report from their agent, Haygood, who, in summation, wrote: "Without *saying it,* I have tried to make the facts say that ours

[1] A. G. Haygood to R. B. Hayes, January 3, 1883, Hayes MSS..

[2] *Ibid.,* February 1, 1883.

[3] Butler, "An Historical Account," p. 78.

is *not the business of an amateur semi-scientific investigating Committee.*"[4] Haygood repeatedly projected the image of a man of action, not one of leisurely study and deliberation.

Based upon Haygood's report, the trustees resolved that schools which "give instructions in trades and other manual occupations" simultaneously with "mental and moral instruction" should be preferred in appropriations of the fund. It was believed that such training would make the students "most useful to their Race."[5] Likewise, direct aid to students would be limited to students who were receiving industrial training together with moral and intellectual training. The board appropriated $20,000 for Negro schools for 1883, directed Haygood to present to the trustees thirty days before the next meeting his observations, conclusions, and recommendations for the further action of the board, and then adjourned.[6]

On August 2, 1883, Haygood delivered a controversial speech, "The Education of the Negro,"[7] at Monteagle, Tennessee, one of the South's leading chautauquas. In his address, Haygood insisted that the Negro had great capacity to learn and that the education of a black child was no different from that of a white child. He believed that a black child of ordinary intelligence can learn just as readily as a white child of ordinary intelligence. He did not propose to assert just how far the Negro could go intellectually, because "nobody knows, even approximately, what he can do." But, "considering what small chance he has had, and the short time in which he has been allowed to learn, his achievements seem to me to be most remarkable."

Haygood believed in educating blacks because he believed in the "essential unity of the human race . . . the brotherhood of the race." Every child, white or black, should have from his parents or from the government an equal chance for elementary education, and

[4] A. G. Haygood to R. B. Hayes, March 3, 1883, Hayes MSS..

[5] A. G. Haygood, *The Case of the Negro as to Education in the Southern States: A Report to the Board of Trustees* (Atlanta: James P. Harrison & Co., 1885), p. 48. Hereinafter cited as Haygood, *The Case of the Negro.* The trustees favored training in the handicrafts because they felt that hand labor built character and helped to abolish poverty. This according to an address delivered by Daniel C. Gilman at the opening of the Armstrong-Slater Trade Building at Hampton Institute, November 18, 1896. D. C. Gilman, "A Study in Black and White," Trustees of the John F. Slater Fund, *Occasional Papers,* No. 10 (1897), pp. 8-13.

[6] The Slater Trustees *Proceedings* (1883), p. 7.

[7] The address is found in A. G. Haygood, *Pleas for Progress* (Nashville: Southern Methodist Publishing House, 1889), pp. 5-24. Hereinafter cited as Haygood, *Pleas for Progress.*

school funds should be fairly and equitably distributed without distinction of race.[8] "Give them all, black and white, the keys of knowledge, and let them unlock as many doors as they can," he declared. Freedmen should be educated so that they might become interested, responsible citizens, not a danger to elections, used by designing white men. The matter was urgent because Negroes were rapidly increasing in numbers. Haygood pleaded for tolerance and help for those (principally northern white missionaries) who were teaching blacks. He acknowledged that there were some "cranks and marplots" among northern teachers, but declared that this was no more an argument against the work itself than "the discovery of an occasional hypocrite and scoundrel in the pulpit an argument against Christianity." He declared it the solemn obligation of southern whites to help black people to help themselves.

Haygood was pleased with the publicity which his speech received and wrote to Hayes that "the speech was one they understood. The Nashville American and the Atlanta Constitution printed it in full." Haygood sent a copy to the New York *Tribune* and found it significant that the *American* endorsed the speech.[9]

About two weeks later Haygood went to Chautauqua, New York, to deliver two speeches on the Negro, the first on "How He Makes His Way."[10] He spoke candidly of his perception of some of the Negro's limitations as a worker and wage-earner and how his lack of schooling left something to be desired in his conduct. He spoke of the Negro's religion, of his loyalty to his church, and of the need of educating the black clergy, and emphasized the need of schools, of lengthening the school term (which was typically three to five months a year), and of strengthening the more advanced black colleges. He urged the people of the North to continue their support

[8] According to Haygood, there was at that time no discrimination in the allocation of school funds except in one state. The United States Commissioner of Education in 1883 reported that, "both races now share alike in the school fund, except in Delaware, Maryland, and the District of Columbia, in which special provision is made for the colored race, and in South Carolina, where the basis of apportionment is the same for each race but the amounts realized depend upon the extent to which the people avail themselves of the provision by absolute attendance upon the schools." *Report of the Commissioner of Education for the Year 1882-83* (Washington: Government Printing Office, 1884), p. lv.

[9] A. G. Haygood to R. B. Hayes, August 4, 1883, Hayes MSS.. The *American* commented in part: "At length the race problem has reached that point, in the process of solution, where it ceases to be considered in its partisan aspect, and it is to be discussed from the standpoint of political philosophy. . . ." Nashville *Daily American,* August 3, 1883.

[10] Both addresses are found in Haygood, *Pleas for Progress,* pp. 25-51 and 55-82.

of black schools in the South inasmuch as southern whites were unable to support black schools while some of their own colleges were being closed for lack of funds. But he confessed that southern whites might have done more to lend support and encouragement to those who were engaged in the work of educating blacks.

Haygood's second Chautauqua address, "A Nation's Work and Duty," was addressed to the problem of financing black education, a national concern, according to Haygood. He commended the work of northern philanthropy in the South and urged federal aid to education distributed to the states proportionally on the basis of the level of illiteracy, as the Blair Bill proposed.

The controversy occasioned by Haygood's speeches interrupted his work and the report on Negro education which he was preparing for the Slater trustees for their meeting in October. The board directed him to send the report to members of the board thirty days in advance of the meeting. Its completion was delayed. Upon its receipt, Chief Justice Waite quizzically wrote to Hayes: "Dr. Haygood has sent me what I understand to be a copy of his report."[11] That Waite might have difficulty recognizing the report for what it was may be explained by Haygood's agitation over the tempest his speeches raised. In a letter to Hayes on September 19, Haygood acknowledged that he was derelict in completing his report and getting it into the hands of the trustees. His excuse was: "I have had the biggest sort of fight in hand since my return [from Monteagle and Chautauqua]." He had published 40,000 copies of the speeches and believed that the discussion which the speeches generated would be beneficial to blacks and to the purposes of the Slater fund.[12]

The Slater trustees met for the fourth time, October 16, 1883, in the Fifth Avenue Hotel in New York City. All but two trustees (Waite and Brooks) were present. They discussed the findings of Haygood's survey of Negro education, including the following informational items:

1. The former slave states have a Negro school population of 1,840,585, of which only 47 percent are enrolled in schools.

2. The average public school term is four months, but the average attendance is only three months.

3. The principal need of black public schools is competent

[11] M. R. Waite to R. B. Hayes, October 14, 1883, Hayes MSS..

[12] A. G. Haygood to R. B. Hayes, September 19, 1883, Hayes MSS..

teachers. Most Negro schools are taught by black women who have insufficient training and skills.

4. In higher grade schools, most of the teachers are whites from the North.

5. Most of the aid being given by southern states to Negro education is in the form of supplemental appropriations to institutions established by churches and benevolent societies; there are only a few public schools for blacks not connected with a church or benevolent society.

6. Only a few Negro institutions fall into the class to which the trustees wish to limit Slater aid.[13]

The general agent recommended to the trustees:

1. Confinement of Slater aid to those institutions found to be most capable of training suitable teachers.

2. Concentration of funds upon a comparatively small number of schools.

3. Fitting the type of aid to the conditions in each school. Thus aid might assume the following forms:

   a. An unrestricted grant.
   b. Support of an instructor in the normal department.
   c. Supplements to salaries.
   d. Payment of the salary of an instructor in the industrial department.
   e. Grants to students.
   f. Purchases of equipment for an industrial department.

The trustees had previously determined during their April 1883 meeting to prefer schools which provided training in manual occupations simultaneously with mental and moral instruction. Since only a few schools met these standards, the board's policy could not be fully implemented until additional school authorities could be persuaded to offer industrial training. When Haygood left the agency in 1891, every school aided by the Slater Fund was offering such training.

After receiving Haygood's report, the board resolved that:

1. A sum not exceeding $1,000 annually would be used as aid to students who show exceptional gifts and promise of usefulness.

2. A sum not to exceed $1,000 annually would be used to aid students of medicine.

3. The general agent was empowered to obligate $20,000 for the

[13] The Slater Trustees *Proceedings* (1883), pp. 9-16.

year ending September 1, 1884, in addition to the remainder (about $4,000) of the $20,000 voted by the board in April for obligation in calendar year 1883.

4. All gifts to a school exceeding $500 would be earmarked for a specified purpose.

5. Aided students, if practicable, will pledge themselves to help their race.

6. It is desirable for aided institutions to raise an amount equal to or greater than the amount of Slater aid for "the same specific purpose."

7. No Slater aid to institutions will be used to pay off debts; nor shall aid be given to schools not believed to be operating on a permanent basis.[14]

Disbursements to schools during the first year of operation of the Slater Fund (that is, to October 16, 1883) totaled $16,250, of which $11,000 went to colleges and universities. Hampton Institute received $2,000 while Tuskegee, a new school, received $100. Secondary schools were awarded $3,150. Colleges and universities receiving aid were: Atlanta, Claflin, Clark, Shaw, and Tougaloo universities and Talladega College. Administrative expenses totaled $3,436.[15]

In January 1884, Haygood reported the first of many differences with the treasurer of the Slater board, Morris Jesup. The latter wished to have more detailed justifications for each appropriation than the general agent was inclined to supply. Haygood complained to Hayes: "How far should I go into details of 'reasons' with Mr. J.? What supervisory relations has Mr. J. or the Finance Committee to appropriations I make?" Haygood asserted that he was neither suspicious nor jealous of authority "but Mr. J's. mental processes I have observed to be peculiar." He doubted the usefulness of putting into Jesup's possession every reason influencing his mind as to appropriations, places, amounts, objects, etc.. His decisions he said grew out of a full year's observation, inspection, travel, correspondence, and conference. Haygood said: "It is not clear to me that I can cause Mr. J. to understand the grounds of decisions."[16]

In his correspondence, Hayes never attempted to act as arbiter between Haygood and Jesup. In the clash over who was to control the expenditure of funds of the agency, Jesup became more

[14] *Ibid.*, pp. 16-18.
[15] *Ibid.*, pp. 19-20.
[16] A. G. Haygood to R. B. Hayes, January 14, 1884, Hayes MSS..

influential than Haygood and was primarily responsible for the growth of the principal of the fund during Haygood's administration from $1,000,000 to $1,185,000,[17] this being accomplished almost entirely by placing income back into the principal. Jesup thus was interested in a strict accounting of expenditures against the fund. Haygood, on the other hand, had a greater interest in grants. And he wished to be free to make grants according to his own lights and resented being put into the role of what he later termed, "the treasurer's traveling man."[18] He did not like to keep detailed records of everything he did and stated that such restraints "would freeze up my soul."[19]

With the president of the board, however, Haygood maintained close ties, confiding in him, flattering him, and seeking his advice and encouragement. Hayes and Haygood had a typical patron-protege relationship as long as Haygood was an employee of the board. In January 1884, Haygood wrote cordially to Hayes: "You did me the honor and favor to give me a photograph of yourself; also one of 'that elect lady,' Mrs. Hayes. I prize them much. You were good enough to ask mine. I send it with pleasure."[20]

On January 14, 1884, Haygood expressed approval of Slater aid for state-supported schools. "Other things being equal," he said, "the state institutions should have as much consideration in the distribution of Slater money as those supported by the churches and benevolent societies." He thought that such aid would help to develop a sentiment among the southern people in favor of the schools which eventually would cause the schools to be completely supported locally.[21] During Haygood's administration of the fund, only six percent of disbursements went to public schools, the niggardliness of the amount being due principally to the scarcity of such schools for blacks. It may be observed, however, with respect to state-supported colleges, there was a bias against such schools among some church men and women, Haygood among them, because it was thought that they could not provide the moral direction needed by their students which church-related institutions provided. This bias was later largely relaxed.

On May 7, 1884, John F. Slater, founder of the fund, died in

[17] The Slater Trustees *Proceedings* (1891), p. 9.
[18] A. G. Haygood to R. B. Hayes, May 20, 1889, Hayes MSS..
[19] *Ibid.,* February 3, 1887.
[20] *Ibid.,* January 30, 1884.
[21] *Ibid.,* January 14, 1884.

Norwich, Connecticut.[22] A short time before his death, he was visited by Haygood. At this time, Haygood later related, Slater stated that the following principles should be followed in the administration of the fund:

1. The fund should encourage practical education under Christian influence.
2. The fund should aid existing schools, not start new ones.
3. The fund should aid schools that train teachers.
4. The fund should help as many schools as possible (thus diffusing its aid).
5. The fund should prefer schools giving industrial training.[23]

These principles, which were articulated by Haygood in his last report as Slater agent in 1891, are those which were followed by Haygood, but which were changed by the trustees when he left. "Christian influence" became less important, and a policy of concentration rather than diffusion was followed in distributing funds. Haygood originally favored concentration, but by 1885 was committed to diffusion.

Early in 1884, D. C. Gilman, secretary of the board of trustees, remarked that the general agent apparently was not as prompt in attending to his correspondence as would be desirable. He acknowledged that he might have been judging incorrectly from a few instances which had come to his attention,[24] but he was not the only trustee who felt the agent was not keeping the members properly informed. In May, Chief Justice Waite inquired: "What has become of Dr. Haygood? I hear nothing of him or his work."[25]

Haygood seemed to be keeping busy, according to his correspondence, although neglecting the trustees. In a letter written to Hayes in June, he asserted that he had travelled thousands of miles and had maintained a constant and widespread correspondence in the interest of the work committed to him. At that time Slater appropriations had been made in Virginia, North Carolina, South Carolina, Georgia, Tennessee, Alabama, Mississippi, Louisiana, and Texas. Haygood said: "Last week I inspected a school in Louisville, Ky.. Two weeks ago I was in New Orleans on the same errand. In a few weeks I shall go to Florida. . . ."[26]

[22] The Slater Trustees *Proceedings* (1884), p. 4.
[23] Butler, "An Historical Account," p. 104.
[24] D. C. Gilman to R. B. Hayes, February 1, 1884, Hayes MSS..
[25] M. R. Waite to R. B. Hayes, May 22, 1884, Hayes MSS..
[26] A. G. Haygood to R. B. Hayes, June 18, 1884, Hayes MSS..

Haygood regarded one of his primary tasks to be to persuade school authorities to accept industrial training. Armed with the power to confer financial support if such training were offered, Haygood was able to realize favorable results from his efforts. Some officials, however, felt that such training was degrading and held out strongly against embracing it. The general agent reported in June 1884 that, with few exceptions, the most skeptical were recognizing the value of industrial work.[27] He said he was heartened by the influence of the Slater Fund in making college work practicable for blacks.[28]

In September Haygood wrote to Hayes and asked to be excused from the Slater board meeting in October. He was helping his sister, Laura, to prepare for her departure to China where she was going as a missionary. His annual report to the trustees was delayed in preparation by the death of Bishop George F. Pierce, senior bishop of the Methodist Episcopal Church, South, who had been Haygood's friend and sponsor for twenty-five years. Pierce had wanted Haygood to supervise the care and management of his papers and literary matters.[29]

The Slater trustees met October 2 in New York City at 52 William Street, Morris Jesup's office. At the suggestion of the finance committee, Slater's initial request that the principal sum of his gift should not be allowed to drop lower than $1,000,000 was considered. The board decided that out of the income of the fund, the sum of $10,000 would be set aside annually as a guarantee against any loss that might arise from investments of the principal. This practice continued until the sum of $100,000 was reached as a guarantee fund. The Board inaugurated the policy by instructing the finance committee, at their discretion, to invest $20,000 in the guarantee fund for fiscal year 1884-85. The trustees voted $40,000 additionally to be appropriated, the sum to be spent according to the principles heretofore adopted by the board. No one institution was to receive more than $2,500 during the year.[30] No reason was given for this additional caveat.

Meeting the next day, Friday, at half past ten in the Fifth Avenue Hotel, their usual meeting place, the board requested the general agent to devote his full time to the work of the Slater Fund rather

[27] *Ibid.*.
[28] *Ibid.*, August 29, 1884.
[29] *Ibid.*, September 19, 1884.
[30] The Slater Trustees *Proceedings* (1884), pp. 6-7.

than to divide it with his presidency of Emory College. Thereupon, Haygood presented a detailed report of the appropriations made to schools to date. A large portion of the $33,000 donated had been spent in building and equipping industrial departments. Haygood believed that a larger portion would be available in the future for salaries and student aid.

Haygood included a report from President E. O. Thayer of Clark University, Atlanta, to the effect that Slater aid helped their printing department where twenty students were taught type-setting and press operation. The shop printed the school's catalogs, a weekly paper, and programs. Thirty students were employed in the carpentry department and constructed eight houses, as well as tables, book-cases, and other furniture. Girls were taught to make dresses for themselves and teachers. The school had a "model house" where girls were taught "house-wifery."

Haygood also reported from President Booker T. Washington that, with Slater aid, students at Tuskegee Institute had made a large part of the half-a-million bricks that were used in construction of their new college building. Young men were taught how to cultivate the soil, prepare manures, and care for stock.[31]

With respect to the board's request that he devote full time to the cause of the Slater Fund, Haygood had been reluctant to sever his connections with Emory College. He had gone into debt in his efforts to help students through school, paying their tuition, buying clothing, and paying their medical expenses.[32] Furthermore, while he had reduced Emory's debt during his presidency, the college's indebtedness remained $25,000.[33]

Upon receipt of the board's request that he devote his full time to the Slater work, Haygood visited each member of the board and apparently persuaded William Slater to pay off Emory's debt of $25,000. He also obtained $3,000 with which to equip a new "Department of Technology" which he wished to install as a result of his interest in industrial training.[34]

Returning from his northern visits, Haygood visited the Negro colleges in Nashville.[35] On November 3 he wrote to Hayes that he

[31] *Ibid.,* pp. 11-14.

[32] Related by several of Haygood's acquaintances in Elam F. Dempsey, *Atticus Greene Haygood* (Nashville: The Parthenon Press, 1939), pp. 43, 53, 142, 255-256, 280. Hereinafter cited as Dempsey, *Haygood.*

[33] Smith, "Haygood," p. 53.

[34] *Ibid..*

[35] A. G. Haygood to R. B. Hayes, October 24, 1884, Hayes MSS..

would begin the Slater work on a full-time basis. He wrote earnestly: "I believe God's hand is in this business. He has opened the way and made it possible and right for me to go forward in it. . . . I write to say I will Jan. 1, 1885, begin on the new basis."[36]

The two years during which Haygood had worked as both Emory College president and Slater agent had been filled with arduous work. Haygood wrote that he worked most of the night when work was particularly pressing.[37] One of his students, who was employed in carrying Haygood's mail to and from his residence and the post office, related that he often had to use a wheelbarrow or a wagon for the outgoing mail.[38] Haygood boasted, after his first month as Slater agent on a full-time basis, that he had returned from a business trip to "find 179 letters to be cared for."[39]

Upon leaving Emory, Haygood addressed an assembly of students at a formal leave-taking on December 16, 1884.[40] He expressed his reluctance to part with the students, but explained that the work into which he was going was much needed. It was a work which "must be done, and a southern man ought to do it." It should be done he thought for the "peace and harmony of the two races."[41] Haygood went into the full-time Slater work with the intention of remaining in it. He wrote: "Now I begin what, if it please God, may take the rest of my active life."[42]

It was agreed by the board that Haygood would receive $5,000 salary and $1,000 for expenses yearly. Hayes, in writing to Gilman of Haygood's terms of employment, said that he was greatly pleased with the new arrangement.[43]

[36] *Ibid.*, November 3, 1884.

[37] Dempsey, *Haygood*, p. 128; George B. Winton, "A Life Sketch of Bishop A. G. Haygood," The Trustees of the John F. Slater Fund, *Occasional Papers*, No. 11 (1915), p. 6.

[38] Related by W. A. Huckabee in Dempsey, *Haygood*, p. 191.

[39] A. G. Haygood to R. B. Hayes, December 22, 1884, Hayes MSS..

[40] Dempsey, *Haygood*, p. lxvi.

[41] Smith, "Haygood," p. 59.

[42] A. G. Haygood to R. B. Hayes, December 6, 1884, Hayes MSS.. Haygood was succeeded at Emory by Isaac Stiles Hopkins, minister, educator, and exponent of technical training, who became the first president of the Georgia School of Technology at Atlanta in April, 1888.

[43] R. B. Hayes to D. C. Gilman, November 11, 1884, Hayes MSS..

# Chapter 4

# Defining the Agent's Role

A few days before beginning his Slater work full time, Haygood wrote to Hayes that he desired the trustees to take an active part in the awarding of appropriations to schools. He asserted that he would be glad not to bear the sole responsibility for appropriating so much money. "It would be a relief to me," he said, "for the Board or the Executive Committee to make the appropriations."[1] The board did not adopt this arrangement until 1887, an arrangement which, judging from his correspondence, Haygood regretted on several occasions.

The Slater trustees met in special session at the Fifth Avenue Hotel in New York City on January 17, 1885, at ten in the morning with only Chief Justice Waite absent. After approving the sum of $500 for clerical services, the board resolved upon a course to "study the condition of instruction among the blacks, in connection with the General Agent, so that the Fund may be useful not only by its direct application but also by its indirect influence."

The trustees wished to "collect, digest, and make known to the public" information about black schools. As a result, Haygood was directed to make a comprehensive report to the board in 1885 relative to the work of Negro education in the South. The trustees made it clear, however, that they wished to get closer to the work in the field than they had been. They suggested that members might accompany Haygood on his visits to schools. They also desired to hear at their upcoming May meeting testimonies of "gentlemen who are known to be in sympathy with this work."

The trustees expressed doubts about the emphasis they had given to manual training and ambiguously resolved that "the Trustees should now take measures to explain what they think is feasible among the schools for freedmen." More specifically, they directed

[1] A. G. Haygood to R. B. Hayes, December 22, 1884, Hayes MSS..

Haygood to report at their next meeting on visits he was to make to schools which provided manual training. Haygood was also requested to secure for each member of the board, copies of catalogs of the schools aided by the fund, together with reports of state commissioners of education and those of educational and missionary agencies working in the field.[2]

On March 10, 1885, Haygood spoke at the dedication of the Elizabeth L. Rust Industrial Home at Rust University in Holly Springs, Mississippi, his subject being "Hand As Well as Head and Heart Training."[3] He reviewed some of the progress which Negroes had made since emancipation, declaring that the most notable advances had been made in education. This should be so, he said, since fifty million dollars had been invested in this cause from philanthropy, taxes in southern states, and the educational division of the Freedmen's Bureau. Haygood insisted that "true education will move along three great lines—books, morals, industry," each type of training reinforcing the others. He believed in this approach to education for whites as well as blacks, and endorsed the Jewish custom of every father teaching his son not only the law and scriptures, but also a trade. He deplored the disposition of some people to be ashamed of hand work, since Haygood believed that hand training could be useful in teaching people the value of work, in quickening the mental faculties, and in helping the individual to approach the ideal of the complete man or woman in his or her personal life. Industrial training was particularly desirable for Negroes, he believed, because they would find employment primarily in industrial occupations. Such training, he said, was the best hope the Negro had of raising his level of living; classical learning by itself could not accomplish the same end. Haygood conceived of Negroes moving from miserable cabins to comfortable housing with the help of hand training.

Haygood, in consonance with the trustees, believed that one of the most important aspects of the Slater work was the development in southern whites of interest in Negro education. In this endeavor, he exerted "prudent and continued pressure,"[4] and he delighted in informing Hayes of progress made. He wrote in March 1885 that the Alabama legislature had increased its appropriation to the Huntsville State Normal School for Negroes from $2,000 to $4,000

[2] The Slater Trustees *Proceedings* (1885), pp. 4-9.
[3] The address is found in Haygood, *Pleas for Progress,* pp. 118-136.
[4] A. G. Haygood to R. B. Hayes, March 21, 1885, Hayes MSS..

annually. He proudly observed: "I have reason to know that the leverage was furnished by our Slater appropriation. The *leaven* does work."[5]

The Slater trustees assembled for their annual meeting at the Fifth Avenue Hotel in New York City on Wednesday, May 20, 1885, at 9 a.m.. Rutherford B. Hayes chaired the meeting which was attended by Chief Justice Waite of Washington, Messrs. William E. Dodge, Morris K. Jesup, and John A. Stewart of New York, and Daniel C. Gilman of Baltimore. General agent Haygood was present as were, by invitation, J. L. M. Curry, agent of the Peabody Education Fund and Gustavus J. Orr, Haygood's friend and Georgia State Superintendent of Schools.

After receiving the report of the general agent, the board heard a report by D. C. Gilman, chairman of a special committee appointed at their extraordinary meeting in January, relative to carrying out the purposes of the board which were resolved at that meeting. Morris Jesup reported on a recent trip he made through the southern states. Curry was heard from in the afternoon relative to Negro education in the South. Orr spoke to an evening session relative to education in Georgia. The board thereupon resolved that appropriations made to schools were for one year only without assurance of renewal. It was also resolved that unused portions of annual appropriations were cancelled at the end of the year.

The board changed its fiscal year's beginning date from September 1 to May 1. The trustees directed their general agent to present on the third Wednesday of each May a budget for the school year beginning in the fall. The board voted an appropriation of $30,000 for the next school year plus an additional $5,000 which might be spent subject to the approval of the finance committee.[6] The board adjourned, not to meet again until May 1886.

In June Haygood wrote glowingly and at length to Hayes expressing satisfaction at signs of progress. He had recently spoken to large crowds ("More southern white people attend than ever before," he said.) in Atlanta, Tougaloo (Mississippi), and Memphis. He related that in Memphis he had an hour-long interview with Colonel Keating, editor of the Memphis *Appeal*. Keating told him "to use his paper as . . . [he] had need."[7]

[5] *Ibid.*, March 5, 1885.

[6] The Slater Trustees *Proceedings* (1885), pp. 10-13.

[7] The *Appeal* was consistently friendly to Haygood in his efforts to aid the Negro. An example of this is found in the paper's comments on Haygood's speech in Holly

Haygood also wrote of his recent visit to Marion, Alabama, where a black school, Lincoln Normal University, was located and at which he spoke: "Many white people attended, the local editor taking me to the school in a carriage. . . . The leading professors of the Baptist University [Judson Female Institute] then called on me & I was urged to deliver an address in the Courthouse to all classes on the subject of Negro education." Haygood related that, ten days after leaving there, the principal of Lincoln wrote him that more Marion people had called to see the school than in all the previous years he had been there.[8]

Haygood repeatedly asserted that the diffusion of Slater money to a great many schools throughout the South was helping to create among southern whites a friendly sentiment for Negro education. Thus he protested when it was suggested that the policy of diffusion be reversed and Slater money be concentrated in a few of the stronger black schools. He wrote that such a policy would "arrest whatever sentiment the Slater work is helping—except in the three or four localities that receive money." He was sure that such a policy would misdirect Slater's aims, since fewer people would be aided.[9]

In the fall of 1885, Haygood addressed the annual session of the Woman's Home Missionary Society of the Methodist Episcopal Church, meeting at Philadelphia, on the subject, "Some Needs of the Negro."[10] He surveyed the general condition of blacks in the southern states. The religious emotions of the Negro were stronger than his moral insights, he said, but charges that the Negro's religion was fanatical were wide of the mark. Moral standards were improving, and he believed that chastity among women was becoming more normative. He referred hopefully to education, saying that he knew of many instances of Negroes helping themselves by building their own schools, or by keeping common schools open for a longer period than public money allowed. The home life of Negroes was poor and meager; most of them lived in one-room cabins, and although they generally displayed apathy toward their surroundings, progress was being made in comfort,

Springs, Mississippi, the previous March 10. The *Appeal's* correspondent wrote glowingly of the address as "one of the ablest, most practical and appropriate addresses I ever heard before any audience here; there was no claptrap, no stilted and fulsome praise, no appeals to the prejudices either of race or section. . . ." Memphis *Daily Appeal,* March 10, 1885.

[8] A. G. Haygood to R. B. Hayes, June 12, 1885, Hayes MSS..

[9] *Ibid.*.

[10] The address is found in Haygood, *Pleas for Progress,* pp. 137-146.

intelligence, and manners. Haygood challenged his audience to greater efforts in missions to southern Negroes, asserting moralistically that only the right use of their (the women's) wealth could make it respectable.

A month following his Philadelphia address, Haygood spoke at the dedication of Morris-Brown College in Atlanta. He spoke on "Building a Christian College,"[11] congratulating the founders of the school on their enterprise. Morris-Brown had been built largely by students under the auspices of the African Methodist Episcopal Church. He advised those in control of the school not to try to pattern the school after Yale, Harvard, or Princeton. He believed that they should be content with modest results until their experience and resources should permit them to operate on a grander scale. He advised them not to go into debt in an effort to build beyond their means. Finally, he emphasized the importance of industrial training, not just for blacks, but for whites as well; and he admonished them to maintain a Christian emphasis in the school.

Following his visit to Morris-Brown, Haygood wrote to Hayes that the new school's property, worth about $12,000, had been earned by the students except for about $500. Still another sign of progress was favorable sentiments among white people: $1,200 had been donated by white Georgians for the purpose of buying grounds in Augusta, Georgia, for Paine Institute. Haygood also reported that the North Georgia Conference of the Methodist Episcopal Church, South, "showed how it thinks better of my work by electing me at the head of its General Conference delegation."[12]

During 1885, Haygood published a report to the trustees of the Slater Fund entitled, *The Case of the Negro As To Education in the Southern States.* In it he reviewed the efforts made in black education both before and after the war. He discussed the work of the Slater Fund, emphasizing the importance of industrial training again and stating that the vast majority of Negro college graduates had become teachers. He reviewed the problems attendant upon educating people just emerging from slavery and asserted his belief that "more and more southern public opinion approves the education of the colored people."[13]

Haygood said that during his first year as Slater agent on a

[11] *Ibid.*, pp. 147-156.
[12] A. G. Haygood to R. B. Hayes, December 3, 1885, Hayes MSS..
[13] Haygood, *The Case of the Negro,* pp. 37-38, 46, 50.

full-time basis, he travelled about 15,000 miles,[14] a remarkable feat in view of the condition of southern transportation systems. Many schools were not on railroads and could only be reached by the most primitive transportation.

During January 1886, Haygood visited schools in Tennessee and Alabama. Booker T. Washington, president of Tuskegee Institute in Alabama, asked him to speak at a mass meeting in Montgomery, Alabama. Promising Haygood a "*very large* audience," Washington explained that the meeting would give colored people the opportunity to contribute to education.[15]

Also in January, Haygood wrote to Hayes of "shortened receipts in this section on account of the low price of cotton." He said that there ought to be some additional Slater money at several of the schools for student aid since a great deal could be accomplished even with small sums: "My experience at Emory while President taught me that very often as small a sum as $20 made the inch of leather that brought buckle and tongue together."[16]

As Slater agent, Haygood received requests for aid in matters not strictly in line with his official duties. He wrote that Negroes from all sections of the country wrote to him for help, "for all sorts of things, building churches, helping to buy farms, running primary schools, & whatever things they can think of." He wrote to thousands of Negroes, he said, "as a matter of education to them, explaining the Slater work & sending information."[17]

On February 8, 1886, Haygood wrote Hayes that Jesup had complained the previous year because the agent's report at the May meeting did not include full details of the disposition of money for the school year ending in June. Haygood replied that the report could not be complete until the school year had been finished. Moreover, in the fall of 1885, Jesup went over the head of the general agent and sent forms to Slater-aided schools by means of which school officials were to make reports directly to the board's treasurer. Haygood complained that Jesup asked many questions of the school officials, "some of which they cannot answer, some of which we have no right to ask." Later Jesup wrote to Haygood that

[14] A. G. Haygood to R. B. Hayes, December 3, 1885, Hayes MSS..

[15] B. T. Washington to A. G. Haygood, January 16, 1886, Hayes MSS.. Later, in 1888, in referring to the work which was being done at Tuskegee, Haygood remarked: "Washington is a very remarkable Negro—a mulatto." A. G. Haygood to R. B. Hayes, October 17, 1888, Hayes MSS..

[16] A. G. Haygood to R. B. Hayes, January 21, 1886, Hayes MSS..

[17] *Ibid.,* February 1, 1886.

he should get reports from schools as nearly like those indicated by his forms as possible. With this, Haygood said he complied.[18]

Another difficulty arose over the issuance of drafts to schools aided by the fund. Haygood issued the second of the three drafts made each year to the schools in February 1886. Jesup then wrote to Haygood that he assumed that the second draft should be issued in January, apparently forgetting (according to Haygood) that the board had specified October, February, and April as the months when payments would be made. The published proceedings of the trustees, however, are silent on a schedule for issuing drafts.

Haygood wrote that he "did not remind him [Jesup] that his attention was specially called to this understanding & that he approved. . . ." Concluding curtly, Haygood declared: "Not in one instance have I intimated a pulse of irritation toward him, nor will I. My letters have been simple statements of fact." Haygood told Hayes that he was sorry to bother him with such matters, but that approval from the president of the board helped him a great deal: "I see not how I could have gone on without it."[19] Haygood added a continuing lament: "I wish much to please—I wish more to do my work properly."[20]

The eighth meeting of the Slater trustees at the Fifth Avenue Hotel on Wednesday, May 19, 1886, found Messrs. Hayes, Waite, Boyce, Dodge, Jesup, and Gilman of the trustees present. The board voted a $40,000 appropriation for the next school year, to be allotted by Haygood. The agent was directed, however, to continue to favor industrial training and to allot up to $5,000 to Clark, Tougaloo, and Shaw universities for the development of exemplary industrial departments. The board further stipulated that no more than twenty percent of the allotted amount should be earmarked for student assistance. Haygood was directed to visit rural communities in the South and report on the conditions of blacks there. He was also directed to make quarterly reports to the trustees "in order that the Board may be informed of any matters of interest."

In furtherance of the goals of the Slater Fund, the proceedings of the meeting and the report of the general agent were printed by the students at Hampton Institute. Previously they had been printed by John Murphy & Company, commercial printers in Baltimore.[21]

[18] *Ibid.*, February 8, 1886.
[19] *Ibid.*.
[20] *Ibid.*, February 12, 1886.
[21] The Slater Trustees *Proceedings* (1886), pp. 3-5.

In October 1886, Haygood spoke at the fourth annual opening of the Gammon School of Theology in Atlanta, Georgia.[22] He praised the northern teachers at the school who had come south to teach the freedmen, a difficult task exacerbated by local opposition and because of its pioneering nature. The hostility of many southern whites who ostracized and otherwise harassed northern teachers could not be justified, he said. But he believed that this state of affairs was changing.

With respect to ministerial education, Haygood noted the tendency of blacks to remove themselves from predominantly white churches and to build their own. He believed that there were elements of immorality and superstition in the religion of the freedmen which served to emphasize the need for schools such as Gammon. He observed caustically that "there is at this time no danger threatening the African pulpit in this country more remote than the danger of over-education."

In November 1886, Haygood conducted the Slater board president, Rutherford Hayes, on a tour of Negro schools in Atlanta. Hayes, who was impressed with what he saw and delighted with the city of Atlanta, had come to preside at a conference of the National Prison Association. Hayes was president of the association, and Haygood, who was also interested in its work, delivered one of the most effective addresses to the conference, according to Hayes.[23] The Georgia prison lease system was one of the principal objects of reform. In September, Haygood had written optimistically of it to Hayes, stating: "The best thought & sentiment of Georgia are dead against it. This feeling grows & the lease system will have to go."[24] Haygood was premature in his optimism. The convict lease system was not outlawed in Georgia until 1907.[25]

Haygood continued his efforts to sell southern white people on the desirability of supporting education for blacks, circulating documents and pamphlets and using the press as opportunity permitted. He wrote that whenever he spoke before an audience he never forgot "the poor Negro." Although these efforts did not show results in verifiable statistics, Haygood considered it imperative that Negro education "take root in the South & in southern white

[22] The address is found in Haygood, *Pleas for Progress,* pp. 175-190.
[23] Williams, *Hayes' Diary and Letters,* Vol. IV, p. 193.
[24] A. G. Haygood to R. B. Hayes, February 3, 1887, Hayes MSS..
[25] Rubin, *Teach the Freeman,* Vol. 1, p. 184.

consciences—else some day it will die."[26] Haygood told Hayes that only someone who had shared his experiences could understand how he thanked God "for the steady, deep change in the feelings of the people. . . ."[27]

At their May meeting in 1886, the Slater trustees directed Haygood to make quarterly progress reports to the board. Haygood, however, showed little aptitude for writing quarterly reports. Nine months later, he protested to Hayes that he had never kept memoranda to show where he was and what he did day by day. If the trustees were afraid that he was not attending to his business properly, he wanted them to know emphatically, *"I have had more advice about overworking than anything else."* He declared that he could not make reports which were "extracts from diaries." Haygood wryly wrote of another of his difficulties in communicating with the trustees: "I believe the best ten days work I ever did for the Negro was while on a fishing excursion in 1883. Then and there," he said, "I made my Monteagle & Chautauqua speeches, intending if I could to force the southern press to discuss the subject. And I succeeded. But what Trustee will understand me when I report '10 days in the woods.' "[28] Although some of the most active board members were dissatisfied with Haygood, Hayes wrote to Gilman in January 1887: "I am entirely satisfied with his work."[29]

The ninth meeting of the Slater trustees was held at the Hygeia Hotel, Old Point Comfort (near Hampton), Virginia, on Wednesday, May 18, 1887, at 10 a.m.. President Hayes was detained by a railroad accident and only took the chair following the presentation and approval of reports of the auditor, finance committee, and the treasurer. The board approved an appropriation ceiling of $45,000 for the 1887–1888 fiscal year and for the first time approved specific apportionments of funds for the institutions the board wished to aid. The trustees resolved that the difference between the $45,000 aggregate and the sum of the specific apportionments could be expended by Haygood after consultation with the president of the board.[30] Thus the agent's hands were effectively tied after several years of discussion of the matter.

[26] A. G. Haygood to R. B. Hayes, January 12, 1887, Hayes MSS..
[27] *Ibid.*, January 7, 1887.
[28] *Ibid.*, February 3, 1887.
[29] R. B. Hayes to D. C. Gilman, January 20, 1887, Hayes MSS..
[30] The Slater Trustees *Proceedings* (1887), pp. 3-6.

# Chapter 5

# Agent Versus Treasurer

At the May 1887 meeting of the Slater board, Haygood, in addition to his customary report on the use of Slater aid, presented a report of a survey which he had conducted concerning certain aspects of the condition of the freedmen.[1] In February he had forwarded about three hundred questionnaires to physicians, clergymen, teachers, lawyers, county officials, school superintendents, merchants, farmers, and mechanics of both races throughout the South. He received two hundred thirty-six replies.

The answer to the first question, "Do colored parents manifest interest in the education of their children?" was overwhelmingly in the affirmative, 229 respondees believing that black parents were interested. Many of the answers were accompanied by qualifying statements, such as: "Not much," "not generally," "to a limited extent," "not as a few years ago," "spasmodic," "some do, some opposed."

Replies to the second question, "Are the common schools attended by colored children improving?" were only slightly less uniform, 196 replying in the affirmative. In every case in which a comment accompanied an affirmative answer, the improvement was attributed to better teachers trained by the colleges and other training institutions for blacks.

Answers to the question, "What are the average wages of common laborers among colored people?" varied widely, although there was sufficient agreement about wages for male farm employees for Haygood to conclude that their average wage was ten dollars a month, food and lodging being furnished. The majority of farm workers, however, worked for a share of the crop.

To the fourth question, "Are the colored people disposed to buy

[1] The report is found in The Slater Trustees *Proceedings* (1887), pp. 3-6, and in Haygood, *Pleas For Progress*, pp. 51-54.

land?" 158 answered in the affirmative. Appended comments, however, generally observed a cityward movement of blacks, who were said to "flock to town because gregarious," or to "go to towns that the women may find employment."

There were 198 affirmative answers to the fifth question, "Are there fewer mulattoes (children with one parent white) born now than twenty-five years ago?" Every Negro answering the question answered "Yes." Twenty respondees said "fewer mulatto births, but more professional prostitution among colored women." Most thought the morals of Negro women had improved.

To the sixth and last question, "Do any considerable number of colored voters side with the Temperance people in Prohibition Contests?" ten replied "Yes, if properly taught;" thirty-seven said "a small percent;" twenty-six said "the better and more intelligent class;" but over sixty answered negatively and only 103 answered affirmatively.

Inclusion of the sixth question in a survey of the condition of freedmen is indicative of the interrelationship of the numerous humanitarian reform movements of the nineteenth century. Of course the overall value of the survey is doubtful. The method by which names were chosen for the mailing list was not provided, nor is there any way to judge the knowledge, experience or biases of respondees. At best, the survey was an opinion poll performed without valid statistical methodology, insofar as the evidence indicates.

In 1887 Haygood spent a busy summer, travelling and speaking frequently. Immediately after attending the Slater board meeting in May, he visited Hampton Institute. On May 20 he was at Franklinton, North Carolina, where he made an address. The next two days, he spoke in the opera house in Raleigh. His subjects concerned a local option prohibition issue and Negro education. In addition, he delivered a sermon in the African Methodist Episcopal Church on black education. He spent the next week at home in Oxford, Georgia, attending to correspondence. On June 1, he delivered the commencement address at Biddle University in Raleigh. That evening he made a local option address at Concord with "white people in front, colored behind." The following evening, he spoke to a large crowd with "colored people in front and white people behind." On June 2 he addressed the pupils of Scotia Seminary, a school for black girls in Raleigh.[2] June 3-10 was spent at

[2] A. G. Haygood to R. B. Hayes, August 9, 1887, Hayes MSS..

home where Haygood attended to office work, correspondence, and the preparation of four articles for publication in *The Advance* and *The Congregationalist* on the Slater work.[3] On the 12th of June, Haygood delivered the commencement sermon at Wofford College, Spartanburg, South Carolina. That evening, he addressed the townspeople of Spartanburg on Negro education. The following week, he attended commencement exercises at Emory in Oxford. On June 25, he delivered the commencement address at the University of Mississippi in Oxford. During the afternoon, he spoke to a group of Oxford blacks and in the evening to the Young Men's Christian Association, an organization in which Slater trustees William E. Dodge, Jr., William A. Slater, and Henry C. Potter were interested.

From July 8 to August 2, Haygood was in Texas speaking on prohibition and Negro education. He considered the trip highly successful and wrote to Hayes that he "did the best month's work I ever did for Negro education." He related that in twenty-five days he made twenty-seven speeches averaging two hours each and preached four sermons. He estimated the size of his audiences at from five hundred to five thousand, averaging two thousand. Most of his speeches were made in opera houses or in the open air. It is not surprising, although Haygood thought it so, that he was exhausted for three days after he returned home, "a thing I never knew before."[4]

In October, Haygood sold his residence in Oxford and bought a "pleasant, modest" home in nearby Decatur, Georgia. He was now within six miles of Atlanta with seven trains daily available to him into the city. He explained to Slater president Hayes that the location was more convenient for his work and left him free of demands on his time emanating from his proximity to the Emory campus in Oxford. His move brought an end to his practice of delivering lectures at night to ministerial students at Emory when he was at home.[5]

Haygood delivered the dedication speech opening the Adeline Smith Industrial Home at Philander Smith College in Little Rock, Arkansas, in March 1888.[6] He urged his listeners not to despise the "day of small things," when their educational resources were

[3] A. G. Haygood to D. C. Gilman, August 10, 1887, Hayes MSS..

[4] A. G. Haygood to R. B. Hayes, August 9, 1887, Hayes MSS..

[5] *Ibid.,* October 18, 1887.

[6] The address is found in Haygood, *Pleas For Progress,* pp. 191-211.

meager, when finances were limited and equipment scarce. They should be thankful for what they had rather than brood about what they lacked, he told them. They should not forget their debt to the people of the North who had established most of the institutions that provided education for blacks. Likewise a debt was owed to white southerners whose taxes supported common schools for Negroes. Haygood advised his audience to take care in the use that they made of their educational advantages, warning that learning makes some people "proud, impudent, lazy, wicked." Such a result, he declared, would tend to turn people against education and arouse vehement opposition. In turn, appropriations for colored schools would likely be minimized, and the schools further hampered in their work. Concluding his address, Haygood congratulated school officials on their industrial program.

In January 1888, Haygood had written to Hayes that the success of "hand" training in the schools caused him to "rejoice and take courage."[7] His travels during the winter of 1888 gave him opportunity to observe the work of a number of industrial departments, and he believed that the zeal of both teachers and students in these departments was increasing. He reported in April that he had visited schools in eight southern states during the winter. "Pardon a scattering letter," he wrote. "This is the fifty-first today on Slater business. I am just home from a three weeks' tour, & day after tomorrow I start on a two weeks' trip." He reported that the schools were more prosperous than at any time during his official connection with them.[8]

The Slater trustees met at the Fifth Avenue Hotel, New York City, on Wednesday, May 16, 1888, at 9:30 a.m.. President Hayes eulogized the board's late vice president, Morrison R. Waite, who died on March 23, 1888. After hearing and approving reports of the auditor, finance committee, treasurer, and general agent, the trustees approved an appropriation of $45,000 for the 1888-1889 fiscal year and stipulated the apportionment of the money as it had the previous year.[9]

The annual report had been printed by students at Hampton Institute the last two years. Secretary Gilman, however, returned the job to a Baltimore printer, William K. Boyle & Son. He was

[7] A. G. Haygood to R. B. Hayes, January 17, 1888, Hayes MSS..

[8] *Ibid.*, April 2, 1888. He had visited South Carolina, Florida, Alabama, Georgia, Louisiana, Mississippi, Tennessee, and Arkansas.

[9] The Slater Trustees *Proceedings* (1888), pp. 3-6.

dissatisfied with the way the job was done at Hampton the previous year.[10] But there is no indication of the source of his dissatisfaction.

Five days after the board convened, James Boyce wrote to Hayes resigning his trusteeship owing to his leaving August 4 "for a protracted stay in Europe. I regret very much not to have been able to render more efficient service than I have," he wrote.[11] The trip was planned to benefit his health. Boyce had failed to attend only one meeting of the board, that in 1885, but when he wrote to Hayes in May 1888, he had attended his last Slater meeting. He died in Pau, France, in December.

The graduation exercises at Claflin University in Orangeburg, South Carolina, were held on May 23 before a large assemblage of white people and blacks.[12] Haygood delivered the commencement address in which he reviewed the progress of black people since emancipation, giving high praise to both blacks and northern philanthropy. Addressing a racially mixed group, Haygood spoke of the obligation of southern white people to aid blacks. He reminded his listeners that many years had passed since the end of the war in 1865 and that there had been sufficient time for people to think clearly and without anger on the past and the problems that it brought. "History," he said, "will blush to record our hardness of heart" if southern white people did not encourage and actively participate in the work of helping the freedmen to help themselves, a matter which was of more concern to southern white people than to anyone else except the freedmen themselves.

Upon reading it, Daniel Gilman, Slater secretary, thought Haygood's address "admirable,"[13] but Haygood felt that the trustees did not really understand his work, particularly his desire to arouse favorable southern sentiment. He wrote Hayes, on whom he continually relied and consulted: "I know the Board. Noble, good men & all that, related to this Slater business in an indefinite sort of way—feeling intense when they think of it, but as to the very thing here in the field—agnostic."[14]

By working in behalf of the public school systems, Haygood believed that he could serve the purposes of the Slater agency. The

[10] D. C. Gilman to R. B. Hayes, February 2, 1887, Hayes MSS..

[11] J. P. Boyce to R. B. Hayes, May 21, 1888, Hayes MSS..

[12] The graduation address and description of the exercises are found in Haygood, *Pleas For Progress*, pp. 212-234.

[13] D. C. Gilman to R. B. Hayes, June 2, 1888, Hayes MSS..

[14] A. G. Haygood to R. B. Hayes, November 1, 1888, Hayes MSS..

question of lengthening the school term in Georgia was being considered by the state legislature and widely discussed throughout the state in the fall of 1888. Henry Grady, editor and publisher of The Atlanta *Constitution*, printed an article on the subject written by Haygood. Haygood believed that if Georgia would improve her public school system, other southern states would follow Georgia's example.[15] Following his delivery of a speech on "The Education of the Masses," Haygood said that he was approached by an Atlanta man, a "Southern Democrat," who told him to put it in pamphlet form, place a copy on the desk of each member of the legislature, "& send [the] bill to him." Haygood added that he sent a copy to every newspaper in Georgia, and expressed the belief that the state would get six-month schools at that session of the legislature.[16]

After speaking at several meetings during the campaign for six-month schools, Haygood, despite being ill, went to Columbus, Ohio, for a meeting of the Freedmen's Aid Society of the Methodist Episcopal Church.[17] Rutherford Hayes attended the same meeting and reported that Haygood made a "wonderful talk. It was humorous, pithy, pathetic, and convincing."[18]

A special meeting of the Slater trustees convened at the Fifth Avenue Hotel, New York City, on Saturday, January 5, 1889, at half past nine in the morning. President Hayes eulogized James Boyce of Louisville, Kentucky, one of the original trustees who had died in December in Pau, France.

The ranks of the trustees were thinning. The resignation of Phillips Brooks, one of the original trustees who had attended only one meeting, was reluctantly accepted. Henry C. Potter, Protestant Episcopal Bishop of New York, was unanimously elected to take Brooks' place. Melville W. Fuller, Chief Justice of the United States, was elected to fill the vacancy caused by the death of Chief Justice Waite.

A suggestion from William E. Dodge, Jr., respecting a possible increase of the fund was referred to a special committee composed

[15] *Ibid.,* November 8, 1888.

[16] *Ibid.,* November 21, 1888. The legislature authorized a gradual increase in the school term: four-month schools in 1889, five-month schools in 1890, and six-month's in 1891.

[17] A. G. Haygood to R. B. Hayes, December 12, 1888, Hayes MSS.. Haygood wrote that he "*nearly* had pneumonia."

[18] Williams, *Hayes' Diary and Letters,* Vol. IV, pp. 429-430.

of Dodge and Daniel Gilman who were to report at the next meeting on the matter.[19]

The matter of replacements for Waite and Brooks had been the subject of exchanges of correspondence between Hayes and Gilman months before the special meeting in January 1889. Hayes wrote in April 1888 to Gilman suggesting Dr. Samuel Green, secretary of the Peabody Education Fund, or J. L. M. Curry, the Peabody agent who subsequently replaced Haygood. Five days later Gilman countered with Potter and Bishop Samuel Smith Harris of Michigan. In May, Hayes wrote again to Gilman, saying: "Seth Low, an Episcopalian of Brooklyn is named to me for the vacancy in a notable way [Melvil Dewey suggested him in a letter of May 19, 1888]. Bishop Potter is surely, however, the man if he will accept it."[20] Low became a trustee after 1900.

Haygood wrote to Hayes in December relative to a replacement for Boyce. "I take it that the Board will elect a Southern man & a Baptist. I suggest Dr. J. A. Broadus. . . ."[21] Two weeks later, Haygood suggested to Hayes that J. L. M. Curry be elected to the vacancy caused by Boyce's death.[22] Two days later, Curry wrote to Hayes and explained that Haygood's reference to himself as a successor to Boyce grew out of his "personal regard for me and because Dr. B. and I belonged to the same denomination [Baptist]."[23] Curry was not elected to the board at this time, but filled another vacancy the following year.

The Slater board convened for its twelfth meeting on Wednesday, May 1, 1889, at the Fifth Avenue Hotel in New York City. The members elected John Albert Broadus to fill the vacancy occasioned by the death of James Boyce. Broadus had succeeded Boyce as president of the Southern Baptist Theological Seminary in Louisville and had been associated with both Boyce and the school for many years.

Reports were heard from the treasurer and finance committee and approved. The trustees approved an appropriation of $45,000 for schools and, upon the motion of Morris Jesup, stipulated that aid to schools was to be approved by the finance committee. Jesup's

[19] The Slater Trustees *Proceedings* (1889), pp. 3-6.

[20] R. B. Hayes to D. C. Gilman, April 18, 1888; Gilman to Hayes, April 23, 1888; Hayes to Gilman, May 23, 1888, Hayes MSS..

[21] A. G. Haygood to R. B. Hayes, December 31, 1888, Hayes MSS..

[22] *Ibid.*, January 12, 1889.

[23] J. L. M. Curry to R. B. Hayes, January 14, 1889, Hayes MSS..

motion took note of the fact that Haygood was not present at the meeting to give information "as to the working of the fund during the past year. . . ." Bishop Potter moved that Haygood be requested to report to the finance committee in advance of each meeting of the board at such time and place as the committee directs.[24]

Although Haygood was not present at the meeting, his report was tendered and printed. His annual reports were detailed, summarizing the amount given and narrating for the trustees the use and results of the grants at each school. His reports concluded with a summary statement relative to the general condition of Negro education, enlightened frequently by extracts from addresses he had delivered. Haygood's audience for his reports was larger than the Slater trustees alone since he sent copies to the press, benevolent societies, school administrators, and others who requested information about the work.

He told the trustees that, since the institutions aided were each different in their circumstances and operations one from another, he believed it was impossible to secure reports from school administrators completed in a simple uniform tabular form. Haygood used a combination of statistics and narrative in his reports. He said he wanted to make the reports helpful to more than the trustees, to administrators and teachers in the schools as well who might be aided by expressions of opinion on subjects by the heads of other schools.

At their May 1889 meeting, the trustees resolved that the Metropolitan Trust Company of New York City would act as financial agent for the trustees for collection of interest from United States bonds held by the trust. Also, that the treasurer be authorized to sell, assign, and transfer federal bonds registered in the name of the trust when the finance committee determines to dispose of the same. The trustees added to the fund's portfolio $85,000 worth of U. S. four percent bonds.[25]

Haygood's continuing efforts in the field brought him both encouragement and consternation. From Holly Springs, Mississippi, where Rust University is located, he wrote that he was grateful for signs that his work was useful in mediating between southern whites and northern teachers in black schools.[26] Consternation arose from Morris Jesup and the finance committee of the Slater board.

[24] The Slater Trustees *Proceedings* (1889), pp. 7-10.
[25] *Ibid.*.
[26] A. G. Haygood to R. B. Hayes, March 23, 1889, Hayes MSS..

The committee met on May 15, 1889, two weeks after the plenary session of the board and drew up several resolutions which they wished the agent to implement. One of the resolutions directed the agent to give notice to the schools that "after the next school year a change may be expected in the method of distributing the Fund looking toward a decrease in the number of institutions aided." Haygood's reaction to this was negative and emphatic: "Of course such notice will practically stop, in schools uncertain as to their fate, any effort at progress that may depend on the Slater Fund." As it turned out, the reduction came in the 1892-1893 school year, the second year after Haygood left the agency.

Another resolution lessened the amount disbursed by the fund by dropping two schools (Mount Albion State Normal School in Franklinton, North Carolina, and Leland University in New Orleans) from the list of schools aided. Haygood objected to the decrease and complained that Jesup never wanted to disburse any unexpended balance, preferring instead to convert it to principal and investing it.[27] When Leland University was discontinued by the finance committee, Edward C. Mitchell, president of Leland, justified himself to Henry L. Morehouse, chairman of Leland's board of trustees, in a collection of letters and reports sent to Morehouse on December 19, 1889. Mitchell bitterly accused Haygood of favoring Methodist schools at the expense of schools sponsored by American Baptists. Haygood countered that, although he was dissatisfied with the work of Leland's industrial department, he recommended continuation of aid thereto but was over-ruled by the finance committee.[28]

Another resolution by the finance committee required the agent to visit each school aided by the fund twice a year and to report on its condition to the trustees. Haygood complained that it would be more beneficial to visit some schools more than twice, while others might receive only one visit or none at all. He wrote to Hayes that the committee's new ruling would force him to travel from 30,000 to 40,000 miles in about ten months. He was appalled at the loss of his independence as a result of the dicta. He felt that his work in gaining a favorable public sentiment and in working for progress in state education had meant nothing to the trustees. The board's policy

[27] *Ibid.,* May 20, 1889. The resolutions, signed by Gilman as secretary, were enclosed in the cited letter.

[28] E. C. Mitchell to H. L. Morehouse, December 19, 1889, and associated papers. Hayes MSS..

declarations were bewildering, he lamented: "If the Agent should attempt to carry out all the unrepealed resolutions of the Board he would work miracles in reconciling contradictions."[29]

Still another resolution of the finance committee had stated that the agent's travelling expenses were to be paid, "of which a separate statement shall be made in detail not limited to the sum of $1,000." This repealed the arrangement made in 1885 by which the agent simply received $1,000 for expenses and did not account for the expenditure of the sum. Haygood questioned the authority of the finance committee to make a new arrangement. He protested that he was not anxious about the money but that he wished to be saved the "irritations" of drawing up itemized accounts. The new arrangement would deny him freedom of movement because he often took trips to speak in behalf of Negro education at places where there were no black schools. "I can never make a man like Mr. Jesup . . . see that the account is for legitimate expenses."[30] This may or may not have been true. The trustees were on record as recognizing the importance of gaining public acceptance of the aims of the trust. Haygood, however, may have seen his mission as Slater agent to be a bit more all-encompassing than Jesup saw it.

Limitations to his freedom of action seemed to disturb Haygood more than anything else. He termed the committee's rulings "a conductor's schedule, not an Agent's work." He protested bitterly against having to get "approval of men a thousand miles away" who knew nothing about his work.[31] Gilman wrote that the members of the board did not wish to have a personal report of how Haygood's time was spent, but that they wanted to be aided in maintaining an intelligent interest in the work being done. He said that he doubted that Haygood "has taken in the idea of a frequent letter." But, he concluded, "I think we must accept him for what he is, & he certainly has unusual excellence, & not for what he is not."[32]

Although Haygood could never bring himself to fully report to the trustees regularly—at least to their satisfaction—his frequent letters to Hayes provide a detailed running account of his activities, which were prodigious as well as hectic. The letters, however, did not document the bases for his decisions to give or withhold aid from schools. Haygood repeatedly wrote that progress was being

[29] A. G. Haygood to R. B. Hayes, May 20, 1889, Hayes MSS..
[30] *Ibid.*, June 8, 1889.
[31] *Ibid.*.
[32] D. C. Gilman to R. B. Hayes, October 19, 1889, Hayes MSS..

made—the schools more prosperous, the climate of opinion more favorable to Negro education, numbers of students increasing, quality of students and instruction improved, and new buildings raised. He undoubtedly had a feel for his work and its results which was not always translated into statistical tables. Members of the finance committee would have preferred the latter. Haygood also had a tendency to paint a more favorable picture than actually existed in terms of developing favorable public sentiment and other goals that he set for himself.

On November 15, 1889, Haygood wrote a second letter to Hayes about the results of the finance committee's latest rulings. The committee's requirement ("without authority," Haygood wrote recriminatively) that he visit each school twice a year had kept him busier than ever. During the past month, he had been in South Georgia, Florida, Mississippi, West Tennessee, and Arkansas, despite his having been ill part of the time. As for the committee's ruling, he said, "I intend . . . to do it & show my desire for harmony."[33]

His dissatisfaction with the action of the committee was not relieved by a letter from Jesup which contained what Haygood construed to be an apology from the treasurer. He wrote to Hayes with apparent sarcasm: "Last night brought a sweet note from Mr. Jesup, in which he comes as near an apology as a man of his kind can, & I wrote him thanking him for his kind note, & I do thank him." But Haygood retorted brusquely: "It cost him enough to excite my gratitude."[34]

[33] A. G. Haygood to R. B. Hayes, November 15, 1889, Hayes MSS..
[34] *Ibid.*, November 1, 1889.

# Chapter 6

# Change and Continuity

On December 11, 1889, Haygood was principal speaker at a memorial service in Decatur, Georgia, for Jefferson Davis, late President of the Confederate States of America, who had died on December 7. In his remarks, Haygood pleaded adroitly for national sentiments while concurrently appealing to the sectional sentiments of his audience. He spoke of Davis' loyalty to the southern people, how he had suffered for them, and of the regret of the people at his passing. As to the Civil War and what had passed since, he urged his listeners to respect facts and be true to the duties of the day as well as to the memories of the past. "Let us cultivate a broad and loyal national sentiment,' he said, "and stand squarely by the Constitution as we have helped to make it. Let us teach our children to love the Union." He declared that both Robert E. Lee and Jefferson Davis did this, and "to do otherwise is lunacy." He was convinced that God had overruled the purposes of the southern people in the Civil War, and he expressed gratitude for the end of slavery and for the restoration of the Union. Concluding, he spoke of expressions of love and gratitude being voiced all over the South for the fallen leader and topped them all with his own sentimental tribute: "As the historian, Motley, writes of the death of William, Prince of Orange, so we may say this day of Jefferson Davis: "And when he died, the little children cried in the streets.' "[1]

On December 25, Haygood and his family moved from Decatur, Georgia, to a new home in Sheffield, Alabama, where he was to become the president of a new girl's school, an adjunct to a real estate development proposed by the Sheffield Land Company. The promoters erected a home for the president and announced its intention to construct a college building costing $50,000. The company also pledged to give $100,000 to endow the school.

[1] Nashville *Christian Advocate,* January 4, 1890.

Haygood was sought by the promoters because they believed he could raise money for the enterprise from among the Slater trustees.[2]

Haygood wrote to Hayes that materially he had little, "not even a home," and that his friends in Sheffield were giving him a home worth about $7,000. Further, the move to Sheffield would be good for his children and would give him the opportunity to "get nearer my own people."[3] Severing his connections with the North Georgia Conference of his church, he resigned his presidency of the board of trustees at Emory and his trusteeship of Wesleyan College.[4]

His bleak financial situation was responsible for his decision to become connected with the Sheffield school. The year before he had asked Hayes for a loan of $600, saying: "I don't wish to seek favor in Atlanta."[5] In 1890 he told Eugene R. Hendrix, a fellow clergyman and future brother in the episcopacy, that he had contracted debts amounting to $15,000 by assuming personal responsibility for some of the needs of Emory College. These debts dated from 1881; in 1890 he still owed $5,000. But to Hendrix he added: "At no time, should I have been called away, would any to whom I owed a dollar lost a dollar."[6]

Nevertheless, Louis Rubin wrote that Haygood defaulted payment on a note to the Fremont (Ohio) Savings Bank, whereupon Rutherford Hayes assumed the obligation. Some years after Hayes' death, the note was paid when Hayes' estate was settled.[7] Late in 1892, Haygood wrote to Hayes explaining his financial predicament. He said he was "on hard times" because his efforts to assume the debts of Emory College "pulverized me." Asserting that when Slater gave $25,000 to cover the debts of the college, it turned out that there were other debts unaccounted for. Haygood apparently was referring to late 1884 when he assumed the Slater agency full-time and endeavored to have Emory's $25,000 debt paid in full through the generosity of the Slater trustees. Here he indicates that William A. Slater (John F. Slater had died in May 1884) had paid the entire debt. As for Emory's other debts, amounting to "several thousand more," Haygood, despite his having stepped down from

[2] Smith, "Haygood," p. 63; Mann, *Haygood,* p. 204.
[3] A. G. Haygood to R. B. Hayes, June 17, 1889, Hayes MSS..
[4] Smith, "Haygood," pp. 26, 35.
[5] A. G. Haygood to R. B. Hayes, December 17, 1888, Hayes MSS..
[6] Smith, "Haygood," p. 43.
[7] Rubin, *Teach the Freeman,* Vol. 2, p. 39.

Emory's presidency, said that he "undertook to . . . meet all. It smashed me," he said, but he hoped by February 1893 to "clear up" his debts.[8] Hayes unfortunately died on January 17, 1893. Despite his efforts to earn money by publication of books and articles in addition to his episcopal salary and the efforts of sympathetic friends to help, Haygood's debts continued to hang over him in his declining years.[9]

In February 1890, Haygood published in the Nashville *Christian Advocate* an article, "Why Peoples Move," in which he commented on the great volume of writing on the race problem: "It is the 'fad' now to solve the Negro Problem," he said. Some people were thinking of getting blacks out of the South. Haygood considered this impractical because he thought blacks did not want to leave, at least not at that time. His rhetorical solution to the problem was unfortunately a simplistic bromide: "Let us have law, education, religion. These solve problems and elevate men. An honest judge—a faithful teacher—a consecrated preacher—these three, working together, can, under God, solve any sort of social and civil problems."[10]

The annual meeting of the Slater trustees was held at the office of the United States Trust Company, of which trustee John A. Stewart was president, at 45 Wall Street, New York City, May 6, 1890. Only four trustees, Hayes, Stewart, Dodge, and Colquitt, were present. Jesup, Slater, and Gilman were absent from the country. Benjamin Strong, Jesup's private secretary, was appointed secretary *pro tem.* Strong was father of Benjamin Strong, Jr., who, at age 18, just out of high school in Montclair, New Jersey, in 1890, was on the threshold of a brilliant banking career. He joined Morris Jesup's banking firm, Cuyler, Morgan & Company, in 1890. He became Assistant Secretary of Atlantic Trust Company in 1901 before joining the Bankers Trust Company as Secretary when the firm was organized in 1903. He became President of the latter firm in 1914, the same year he was appointed first Governor of the Federal Reserve Bank

[8] A. G. Haygood to R. B. Hayes, November 7, 1892, Hayes MSS..

[9] Mann, *Haygood,* p. 208. Replying to a letter from Haygood from Los Angeles dated August 8, 1891, Hayes wrote of his own financial straits closing with: "You see the situation and will do what you can, I know. Your case is only a drop in the bucket. . . . So do the best you can and be easy in your mind. Our friendship will suffer no strain, whatever the result. I shall always be grateful that it fell to me to make your acquaintance and enjoy your friendship." R. B. Hayes to A. G. Haygood, August 24, 1891, Rubin, *Teach the Freeman,* Vol. 2, pp. 207-208.

[10] A. G. Haygood, "Why Peoples Move," Nashville *Christian Advocate,* February 15, 1890.

of New York. Strong had a positive and dominant personality. He died of tuberculosis in New York City in October 1928.

The trustees heard and approved the treasurer's and finance committee's reports and appointed William Slater auditor to examine the assets of the trust. W. H. Hickman, president of Clark University in Atlanta, reported on efforts to make Clark's industrial department an example to other schools, with the aid of Slater funds. Pleased with what they heard, the trustees thereupon converted a $1,500 loan to the university to a grant, on motion of John Stewart. Haygood delivered his annual report, a bit shorter than usual, and recommended that an additional sum of $6,490 be appropriated to be divided among twenty-three beneficiaries. On motion of William Dodge, the appropriations of 1889 ($45,000) were continued for the coming year, and the additional amount requested by Haygood was granted. A suggestion of the finance committee was heard and referred back to the committee and the president for action. The suggestion was that a "more practical and efficient business method" for distributing the gifts of the fund and for obtaining greater knowledge of the work of the fund and its results should be formulated. Benjamin Strong was then directed to arrange for publication of the annual report.

Haygood supplemented his report with a statement, containing examples, of how Slater aid prompts others—private citizens, associations and state legislatures, to assist in supporting black schools. He further reported (on July 4, 1890) how the southern press had reported favorably on commencement exercises held at Slater-aided institutions.[11]

On Monday, May 19, 1890, the General Conference of the Methodist Epscopal Church, South, meeting in St. Louis, elected Haygood, for the second time, to the office of bishop. He was elected on the first ballot with 171 votes, 137 being necessary for election.[12] The vote was the largest ever given a bishop-designate in his church. His election was attended with great enthusiasm. Haygood was delighted with his second election to the office because he had been criticized for declining consecration in 1882. This time he accepted. Hayes termed the election an "immense personal triumph."[13]

Haygood wrote glowingly on June 2 that the "younger and progressive" bishops were insistent that he continue his Slater work.

[11] The Slater Trustees *Proceedings* (1890), pp. 3-6, 24-29.

[12] Nashville *Christian Advocate,* May 31, 1890.

[13] A. G. Haygood to R. B. Hayes, June 11, 1890, Hayes MSS..

He believed it possible that he could fill both offices concurrently and outlined a plan whereby the next year could be managed "without the least difficulty." He said he had only five church conferences to hold, two in Mexico (taking two weeks) and one in Texas. Going to Mexico, he went by three of the Slater-aided schools in Little Rock, Waco, and Austin. Returning from Mexico and Texas, he held a conference in Louisiana. This trip took him through New Orleans where two of the schools were located. From there he could easily make a circuit through Memphis, Nashville, and Atlanta, finally going to Macon, Georgia, where he held his last conference on December 17. After Christmas "I go preaching pretty much where I please. It is easy to spend a Sunday in Columbia, Raleigh, Richmond, Charlotte, Montgomery, & the Monday in our school. . . ." Haygood said that Bishop Charles B. Galloway had offered to help him, to go with him to see many of the schools. He added, however, that "if the Board desires it I will of course get out of the way of any plans they have. . . . As to what is after next May," he concluded, "we will confer."[14]

Hastily changing his mind, a week later he wrote that he did not wish to keep the agency after it was thought best to make other arrangements. He again expressed confidence that he could handle the remainder of the year already entered upon (1890-1891). If this were done, he wished to prepare a resume reviewing in one final statement what the fund had sought and what it had accomplished during its first nine years. Concluding his letter, he declared: "You will not think that my consenting to ordination [sic] means the least decadence of interest in the uplifting of the Negro."[15]

Sentiment which favored Haygood's continuation in the work was expressed to Rutherford Hayes, Slater president. Besides some of his episcopal colleagues, George W. Hubbard, dean of Meharry Medical College in Nashville, expressed the hope that he would continue. He believed that he expressed "the general sentiment of those who have charge of the institutions assisted by the fund, when I say that it is very desirable that he still retain the general supervision of the work that he has so successfully conducted in the past." He suggested that, in view of the fact that he could not devote all of his time to the work, some arrangement might be made by

[14] *Ibid.*, June 2, 1890. Galloway later became a trustee of the Slater Fund.
[15] *Ibid.*, June 11, 1890.

which Haygood could have an assistant to act under his supervision.[16]

The governor of Alabama, Thomas Seay, expressed the hope that Haygood would not sever his connection with the Slater fund. Referring to him as "the wise, brave Christian in whose advance criticism itself has been shamed into silence," he wrote to Hayes, "I assure you, My Dear Sir, that in my judgement there is no one in the entire country in whom . . . there unites so much confidence."[17]

Haygood's first reaction to being elected to the episcopacy, that he could handle both the Slater agency and his episcopal duties, may have sprung from his financial straits. He was still deeply in debt. On the other hand, while in 1885, Haygood had said that he hoped to continue his Slater work for the rest of his life,[18] there are indications that he may have had a change of heart. His friend, W. P. Lovejoy, who visited him early in 1890, wrote that in their talks on that visit, Haygood talked mostly about the church and his interest in its organization and work, but said nothing about his Slater work.[19]

The trustees apparently were ready to cut their ties to their agent and made no overtures to him to stay. Haygood sent two resignations to the president of the Slater trustees in September 1890, one to take effect the following May, the other to take effect at the board's convenience, "so that you will save me from being asked out."[20]

Shortly after Haygood's elevation to the episcopacy, consideration was given to his replacement in the Slater agency. Lyman E. Prentiss, pastor of the First Methodist Church in Knoxville, Tennessee, inquired of Hayes about the impending vacancy.[21] Howard Henderson, a lawyer, cleric, and former superintendent of education in Kentucky, wrote to Hayes applying for the job.[22] As early as September 11, 1890, Hayes showed a preference for J. L. M. Curry. Writing to Gilman, he pointed out the advantage of selecting the Peabody agent: "We can save largely in salary and get a capital man. . . ." Asking Gilman to "think of it and let me know how it strikes you," Hayes added that he wanted the trustees from the South—Broadus and Colquitt—to be present when Haygood's

[16] G. W. Hubbard to R. B. Hayes, June 18, 1890, Hayes MSS..
[17] Thomas Seay to R. B. Hayes, June 20, 1890, Hayes MSS.
[18] A. G. Haygood to R. B. Hayes, December 3, 1885, Hayes MSS..
[19] Dempsey, *Haygood,* p. 491.
[20] A. G. Haygood to R. B. Hayes, September 17, 1890, Hayes MSS..
[21] L. E. Prentiss to R. B. Hayes, June 7, 1890, Hayes MSS..
[22] Howard Henderson to R. B. Hayes, November 14, 1890, Hayes MSS..

successor was chosen "as that would enable us to select a man who can reach their section."[23] In reply Gilman wrote that he was favorably disposed toward Curry "provided that we can supplement him with a younger person [Curry was 65] particularly well qualified to go from place to place and show the right methods of manual training." Gilman was not concerned with saving money on his salary. He wanted to get the job done—"promote the right kind of instruction among the blacks."[24]

In October Hayes wrote to Gilman that he had seen Jesup in New York, and Jesup wanted to employ Andrew Sloan Draper, New York State Superintendent of Public Instruction, as agent. Hayes gave the impression that Jesup was "strongly inclined against taking an agent from the Peabody fund," and that Jesup spoke not only for himself, but for the other New York trustees, Stewart and Dodge, as well. As for Draper, Hayes believed it would be "a serious mistake to appoint an Agent not specially acceptable at the South." With respect to Curry's appointment, Hayes wrote: "The opposition of the N. Y. men can be removed, I think."[25]

It may be remembered that Hayes had ties to Curry which went back to their Harvard Law School days in 1843 when the two were not only classmates but shared lodgings in Cambridge. As President of the United States, Hayes had offered Curry a cabinet post which the latter declined. They were both trustees of the Peabody Education Fund.

Just prior to the October 1890 meeting of the Slater trustees, Moses Pierce, former neighbor of the late founder of the fund, who was a trustee of Hampton Institute and benefactor of black schools, wrote to Hayes to recommend Joseph E. Roy as Haygood's successor. Roy was employed by the American Missionary Association and had been considered as agent in 1882 when the fund was established.[26]

The Slater trustees met at the Fifth Avenue Hotel in New York City, Wednesday, October 29, 1890, at 10 a. m.. All the trustees were present except Chief Justice Fuller. On motion of Henry Codman Potter, it was resolved to accept Haygood's resignation to take effect at the next annual meeting in May. On motion of John Stewart, a committee consisting of Hayes, Jesup, and Gilman was appointed to

[23] R. B. Hayes to D. C. Gilman, September 11, 1890, Hayes MSS..
[24] D. C. Gilman to R. B. Hayes, September 16, 1890, Hayes MSS..
[25] R. B. Hayes to D. C. Gilman, October 10, 1890, Hayes MSS..
[26] Moses Pierce to R. B. Hayes, October 28, 1890, Hayes MSS..

consider and recommend action to be taken to fill the vacancy caused by Haygood's resignation. The board then recessed until 3:30 p. m..

Upon reassembling, the committee recommended and the trustees approved the abolishment of the position of general agent. In its place the board established an educational committee consisting of six trustees, three of whom were to be appointed by the board while the other three were to be *ex officio* members—the president, secretary, and treasurer.

The duties of the committee were:

1. To study the education of American Negroes.
2. To visit schools aided by the fund.
3. To select a person to aid in the promotion of manual training under the direction of the committee or the board. To set compensation for this person.
4. To report in writing at the board's annual meetings on the educational and related work of the fund.
5. To meet at least four times during the year.

The board resolved that the chairman of the committee would receive compensation to be set by the board. In effect, he was to act as the general agent of the trustees, but as a trustee, not an employee. The board then proceeded to elect a new member, J. L. M. Curry, agent of the George Peabody Fund. Curry was chosen to chair the committee, while Colquitt and Broadus were chosen members to act with the chairman and the three *ex officio* members.[27]

Thus the board moved swiftly to insure no loss of momentum in their work and to chart new courses of stewardship for themselves as they prepared to sever relations with Haygood and entered upon a new phase in the life of the foundation.

The change began smoothly. In late November, Curry wrote to Hayes of his visit to New York where he had a "very pleasant and satisfactory interview with Mr. Jesup," who, we are told, received Curry cordially and, with a sense of urgency, asked him to accept the chairmanship of the board's educational committee and to begin immediately the discharge of its duties. The previous evening, Curry had been with Daniel Gilman in Baltimore in "a full and free consultation" which was entirely satisfactory to Curry. "Their opinions and reasons, coinciding with yours," he wrote, "I decided, with some hesitation but with the highest appreciation of the honor,

[27] The Slater Trustees *Proceedings* (1891), pp. 3-6.

to accept and enter at once upon the discharge of the duties of the position." It was understood by each of them, that Curry's acceptance would not interfere with Haygood who would continue to serve as agent until the board met in May 1891. Curry also reported the ready assent, except for Senator William M. Evarts, of the Peabody trustees to committal of the administration of the trusts to the same person, all the while keeping the interests of the Peabody and Slater foundations separate and independent.

Curry reported to Hayes that A. D. Houghton of Atlanta University had been tentatively appointed agent of the Slater education committee with a salary of $1,500 annually. Curry requested Hayes' concurrence in the appointment and mused, "Shall I order a little Slater Fund Stationery—"[28]

As to his successor, Haygood suggested W. H. Hickman of Clark University in Atlanta, who, said Haygood, knew the work well and had particularly good understanding of industrial education. Haygood considered Curry "able and wise," but, because of his age, thought he might be hampered in travelling.[29] Later Haygood asserted that Curry would be the right man for the work because, he thought, Curry "would hold the grip we have in the South."[30]

The advantages of combining the work of the Peabody and Slater agencies had been suggested by Haygood as early as December 1885 when the Peabody agency became vacant as a result of Curry accepting appointment as Minister Plenipotentiary to Spain. Both fund's covered the same field and sometimes helped the same schools; the agents travelled the same territory and visited the same places; they had to know the same school laws and dealt with the same officials. Moreover, the Slater agent might get a more sympathetic hearing from the whites in his appeal for aid for Negro schools, if he, as Peabody agent, could help white schools. Furthermore, the administration of each fund was similar. And economy accrued in travelling expenses and salaries for the agents.[31]

Curry recognized the advantages and, when he learned of Haygood's acceptance of the office of bishop, wrote that "it is a pity that Peabody & Slater are not under the same agency." Next to that,

[28] J. L. M. Curry to R. B. Hayes, November 26, 1890, Hayes MSS..

[29] A. G. Haygood to R. B. Hayes, September 17, 1890, Hayes MSS..

[30] *Ibid.*, October 3, 1890.

[31] *Ibid.*, December 14, 1885. Haygood wrote to Hayes in strictest confidence to suggest advantages accruing from a joint Peabody-Slater agency and expressed a willingness to take the job.

however, he declared, was the "cordial cooperation of the agents." His association with Haygood had been pleasant, he said: "With Dr. Haygood our work goes on harmoniously & effectively & I should be much handicapped if my colleague, so to speak, were a narrow, obstinate, pigheaded fanatic. It is a delight to work with Haygood."[32]

The administrative union of the two funds was announced in a circular addressed "To the Correspondents of the Slater Trustees," which was distributed by secretary Gilman on December 30, 1890. The circular explained that the trustees had invited J. L. M. Curry "to assume the duties which Dr. Haygood will relinquish in May."[33]

A similar union took place in 1903 following Curry's death when Wallace Buttrick, agent of the General Education Board, became agent of the Slater trustees.[34] Until 1902, Buttrick had a career as a railway mail clerk (briefly) and Baptist clergyman. A graduate of the Rochester Theological Seminary in 1883, he served as pastor of churches in New Haven, Saint Paul, and Albany. In 1902 he was chosen the first secretary and executive officer of the General Education Board established by John D. Rockefeller that year. The remainder of his career was spent in education. He died in 1926.

During the last year of his Slater work, Haygood became increasingly involved in the work of the church. Nevertheless, he wrote to Hayes in October 1890 that he had not spent one minute of the board's time in the interest of the Sheffield school. He related that at that time not even a charter or a board of trustees had been obtained for the school.[35] It was understood by the trustees, however, that he would perform his episcopal duties concurrently with his Slater duties. Thus during the fall of 1890, he presided at conferences in Mexico, Texas, Louisiana, and Georgia.[36] Curry wrote to Hayes in January 1891 that Haygood was so busy with his "arduous episcopal functions" that he had not replied to his inquiries.[37]

[32] J. L. M. Curry to R. B. Hayes, June 2, 1890, Hayes MSS..

[33] "To the Correspondents of the Slater Trustees," December 30, 1890, Hayes MSS..

[34] The Slater Trustees *Proceedings* (1903), p. 5.

[35] A. G. Haygood to R. B. Hayes, October 13, 1890, Hayes MSS.. In March 1889, Haygood told Hayes of the forthcoming publication of his book, *The Man of Galilee,* and explained: "It was written nearly all of it before I heard of Mr. Slater. It was copied and revised a year & more ago, a little at a time, in my bedroom at hotels on my trips. I want to say this, that it may not be supposed I have done literary work at the expense of my agency." A. G. Haygood to R. B. Hayes, March 23, 1889, Hayes MSS..

[36] Smith, "Haygood," p. 71.

[37] J. L. M. Curry to R. B. Hayes, January 10, 1891, Hayes MSS..

During the last months of his Slater connection, Haygood arrived at the conclusion that much of his trouble with treasurer Jesup had been caused by Jesup's private secretary, Benjamin Strong, Sr.. He told Hayes that Strong had repeatedly caused trouble over bookkeeping. He wanted schools to send in "itemized statements in advance of expenditures." He was "constantly teasing [A. D.] Houghton [superintendent of the industrial department at Atlanta University] about the *method* of book-keeping. . . ." Strong, he said, had "repeatedly during the year undertaken to lecture & direct me as well as our Atlanta friends. Him I do not answer except as I have business."[38] On this rather acid note, Haygood's relations with treasurer Jesup ended.

[38] A. G. Haygood to R. B. Hayes, November 28, 1890, Hayes MSS..

# Chapter 7

# The Haygood Era: Summary of Slater Fund Management

Haygood finished his final report to the trustees on April 30, 1891, while he was in Orangeburg, South Carolina, to deliver the commencement address at Claflin University, his "closing official function in the agency." He expressed gratitude that the agency had given him the opportunity to speak to blacks often, estimating that since 1882, he had spoken to blacks not less than four or five hundred times. "Providence has kept me safely in long journeys," he said; "I think one hundred and fifty thousand miles I have travelled in this ministry."[1]

The Slater trustees met at the office of the United States Trust Company in New York City on Wednesday, May 20, 1891, at 11 a. m.. All trustees were present except Bishop Potter and Chief Justice Fuller. A telegram from Haygood was received and read after which a minute with respect to his services was read and approved. The board approved $50,000 recommended by the finance committee for expenses during the following year in addition to $800 for clerical aid for the treasurer, Jesup.

Curry, as chairman of the education committee, presented his report, and a minute was approved for the information of the public relative to the change occasioned by Haygood's resignation. It was explained that hereafter the board would concentrate funds on a few schools "which especially deserve encouragement." In deciding which schools to aid, the board would be guided by:

1. Geographical location.
2. Efficiency with which the schools are operated.
3. The service they render in training teachers, and

[1] A. G. Haygood, "A Long and Weary March," Nashville *Christian Advocate,* May 9, 1891.

4. Efforts they make in promoting industrial education.

The trustees thereupon appropriated $47,000 for the 1891-1892 school year, stipulating as the board had done previously that recipients should understand that the aid was for one year only with no assurance of renewal, a stipulation similar to late twentieth century zero-base budgeting.

Curry, in his first report as chairman of the education committee, asserted the following statements of purpose:

1. Slater aid, being limited, should be concentrated on a few schools which could produce superior results, the latter serving as exemplars to other schools.
2. Funds should be concentrated on teacher and industrial training.
3. Aid should be given for the purpose of "lifting up" women in order to improve home life and purify society.
4. Student aid is of low priority and should be discontinued.
5. Slater funds should be used to pay salaries of teachers engaged in normal and manual training.
6. The trustees should publish from time to time studies growing out of the educational work of the trust.[2]

With respect to the last recommendation, the trustees began the publication of a series of "Occasional Papers."

During its first nine years of operation, the Slater board disbursed approximately $322 thousand for Negro education (see appendix C). The most frequent uses of the money during the period 1882-1891 were:

1. Salaries of instructors in industrial and normal departments.
2. Purchase of equipment, almost always in industrial departments.
3. Construction of buildings, usually to house industrial departments.
4. Purchase of supplies, usually for industrial departments.
5. Wages for student labor.
6. Scholarships.
7. College administrative expenses.
8. Printing.
9. Purchase of library books.[3]

Few students in the colleges and universities aided by the Slater Fund were actually performing college-level work. In Haygood's

[2] The Slater Trustees *Proceedings* (1891), pp. 7-11, 12-27.
[3] Butler, "An Historical Account," p. 115.

survey of Negro education in 1885, he reported that less than five percent of the 8,000 students in these schools were performing on the college level. As late as 1916 when Thomas Jesse Jones made his sweeping survey of Negro education, only three schools, Fisk, Meharry, and Howard, could be characterized as "colleges" considering qualifiers such as adequacy of student body, faculty, equipment, and income. Only 33 of the 653 existing private and state schools for blacks were teaching *any* subjects of college grade.[4] Most of the students in 1885 had been preparing to become elementary school teachers, requirements for which tended to be minimal. Most who graduated from the few advanced schools either became clergymen or teachers.[5]

The Slater trustees thought that aid to Hampton and Tuskegee institutes was unusually useful. These schools were specialists in industrial training, Hampton having been the early leader in the field. These schools trained hundreds of manually trained graduates who went into teaching jobs. Most of the Slater aid to these schools went toward salaries for industrial instructors.[6]

Many of the private secondary schools helped by Slater appropriations were semi-public. Local authorities often gave public support to schools established by northern missionaries in lieu of establishing separate public schools for blacks. Slater aid in such schools went toward paying salaries of industrial training instructors and to purchase equipment. Aid to these schools ceased a year after Haygood left the agency because of the trustees' policy of concentrating disbursements. Slater aid was resumed in 1901.[7]

Concentration versus diffusion of Slater aid was discussed among the trustees and their agent for a number of years. By 1885 Haygood favored diffusion and said that John F. Slater had favored it. He regarded it as a tool to get more widespread local support for black schools. It was a form of pump priming, as Haygood viewed it. He was supported by W. D. Godman, principal of Gilbert Seminary, Winsted, Louisiana, in a letter to Hayes in 1888. Godman extolled the diffusion principle as "working wonderful results . . . [and] destined to produce future results of inconceivable magnitude." He seemed to feel that the diffusion of funds brought schooling to

[4] Charles S. Johnson, *The Negro in American Civilization* (New York: Henry Holt & Co., 1930), p. 288.

[5] The Slater Trustees *Proceedings* (1886), p. 41.

[6] Butler, "An Historical Account," p. 118.

[7] *Ibid.*, pp. 119-120.

where prospective students were, and that accessibility was more beneficial than a few large, better-equipped schools.[8]

Curry took a different view, as chairman of the Slater board's education committee. After studying responses to a circular sent to "Correspondents of the Slater Trustees" by secretary Gilman, Curry wrote to Hayes that "diffusion is weakness; concentration on selected schools and objects is strength." While Curry believed that all of the private denominational schools performed beneficial work, a few were "very valuable."[9]

In November 1891, a six-state tour of eighteen Slater-aided schools in company with Hayes confirmed Curry's preference for concentration. He wrote that he was disappointed in the industrial training offered by the schools. He found it unsatisfactory and misrepresented in the school catalogs. The instructors were often incompetent and lacking in general education and well-roundedness. While concentration seemed necessary, Curry recognized the problems inherent in the change of policy. ". . . The practical problem of selection is more difficult than I had imagined—and when made will excite much local and sectarian criticism and censure. . . ."[10]

The trustees' reversal of policy from diffusion to concentration raises some interesting questions about the effects thereof in view of southern political developments in the 1890's, the rise of Populists, and their attitudes toward education for blacks. Did the policy reversal destroy the influence of diffusion in gaining the support of southern whites for Negro education? Would the reverses suffered by Negro education in the 1890's and early 1900's have occurred had black schools in great numbers continued to provide manual (vocational) training? Would it have been more difficult for Populists to have deprived black schools of money if the diffusion principle in Slater aid had been continued in the 1890's? An answer to these questions is necessarily speculative, but if there were validity to Haygood's repeated reports of heightened local interest in black schools during the period of his Slater connection, one may assume that the severance of Slater aid ties to local communities with its emphasis upon vocational training may have caused people to forget and produced indifference to the cause represented by the Slater grants.

[8] W. D. Godman to R. B. Hayes, April 12, 1888, Hayes MSS..
[9] J. L. M. Curry to R. B. Hayes, April 8, 1891, Hayes MSS..
[10] *Ibid.*, November 27, 1891.

Slater aid to state normal schools (1882-1891) was used chiefly for salaries of industrial instructors. Inclusive of money given to Tuskegee, which was a state normal school until 1904, aid to these schools totaled $20,200 under Haygood's management.[11] Little aid went to public schools because there were few which met the requirements of the board for aid. Direct grants to students were always small, never exceeding $550 annually, although payments to students for labor performed was a common use of Slater funds. The latter was administered by the schools and never exceeded 20 percent of annual Slater appropriations. Initially both Haygood and the trustees desired to help promising young black students to further their education, but such help was discontinued after he left the agency, again because of the policy of concentrating funds in a few schools.

Of the $321,990.76 disbursed by the Slater Fund for educational purposes during the first nine years, $298,750.76, or 92.8 percent, went to private secondary and higher education; $19,290, or 1.2 percent, went to miscellaneous projects. Under Haygood's successor, Curry, the amount going to public schools rose slowly, while aid to Hampton and Tuskegee also increased. Under Haygood, 9 percent of the aid went to these two schools. But under Curry, 36.7 percent went to them. Aid to colleges and universities was reduced proportionally (from 62.4 percent of the total to 51.5 percent) under Curry.[12]

Administrative costs were high during Haygood's management of the fund. The average annual cost was $6.2 thousand which represented 14.5 percent of the total disbursement. The principal reason for the high administrative costs is that Haygood's entire salary and travel expenses were paid by the Slater board whereas his successors were in the employ of other foundations which shared these expenses. The policy of diffusion also resulted in higher travel costs (see appendix B).

The trustees insisted that each grant be made with no guarantee of renewal. The board believed that an institution might look upon a yearly Slater grant as a part of its fixed income. Nevertheless, a number of schools were aided year after year with singular regularity.

During the first nine years of the Slater Fund's existence, the board of trustees had two standing committees, the executive and

[11] Butler, "An Historical Account," p. 122.
[12] *Ibid.*, pp. 113, 450.

the finance. The former originally (1882) consisted of Hayes, Colquitt, Dodge, Boyce, and Gilman. Upon Dodge's death in 1883, Chief Justice Waite was added to the committee. Phillips Brooks was added in 1884 but was never active. Boyce died in 1888, and Brooks resigned in 1889, but no one was added to the committee until 1891 when both Broadus and Potter became members (see appendix D).

There were fewer changes in the finance committee, the more powerful of the two committees. It originally (1882) consisted of Stewart, Dodge, and Jesup. Upon Dodge's death in 1883, his son was named to replace him. There were no other changes until 1903 when William E. Dodge, Jr. died.

The finance committee acted as an educational committee prior to 1890 when a separate education committee was formed. Members were desirous of being apprised closely of the work in the field. They showed their dissatisfaction when Haygood failed to keep them informed as they wished. They requested quarterly reports as well as annual reports. They wanted to know detailed reasons affecting Haygood's decisions to confer or withhold grants. In 1887 they began the practice of approving grants before they were made. At other times, they limited the agent's authority in other ways.

Haygood balked at preparing quarterly reports and despaired of making committee members understand the reasons for his decisions. He wanted the authority and responsibility for conducting a grants program based upon his knowledge of black education. He seemed no little exasperated when members of the finance committee did not have sufficient confidence in him to simply more or less acquiesce in his decisions.

Haygood's biographer, Harold Mann, believes that Haygood's health began to fail in 1887.[13] His efforts as author, public speaker, advocate, and itinerant were herculean and possible only to a highly motivated and physically vigorous person. They left him little time to attend to the nagging requests of the finance committee. Haygood was further drained by personal debt and the care of a wife whose health was chronically delicate. Four years after leaving the Slater agency, after living in Los Angeles, California, until 1893, then back in Georgia, Haygood died on January 19, 1896, following a stroke at the age of 56, burned out with his episcopal and literary efforts. In death, he was not forgotten by the Slater trustees who

[13] Mann, *Haygood,* pp. 201-211.

paid tribute to him at their next annual meeting. In 1915, the trustees published "A Life Sketch of Bishop A. G. Haygood" in one of their *Occasional Papers.*

The trustees established an education committee in 1890, as we have seen, the chairman of which was J. L. M. Curry. At the same time, they abolished the position of general agent. Curry's position as a trustee and chairman of the education committee gave him influence on the governing board which was invaluable to him as well as to the trustees.

Since Haygood had not been a member of the board, his position was weakened. At critical moments, he became, or appeared to become, an alienated employee of the trustees, both an illogical and intolerable situation from his point of view. Had the agent occupied a position on the board, much of the friction between Haygood and the finance committee might have been avoided. Had Haygood been more attentive to attending meetings of the board (he was present at 6 of the board's 15 meetings during the period 1882-1891), he likely would have been more aware of the trustees' interest in his decisions, and the trustees would have been more inclined to treat Haygood as one of them.

As for his qualifications to act as the Slater trust's first agent, Haygood had administrative and public relations experience as president of Emory College, skill as a writer and speaker, recognition in the southern states, and demonstrated interest in the objectives of the fund. He was an educator bent upon an educational task in a field requiring the exercise of critical faculties. Foundations continue to favor candidates for staff positions who come from academe, usually with administrative experience.

Haygood was impatient of inaction and staff work when he regarded it as unnecessary. Thus his personality was the opposite of the successful bureaucratic functionary. He authored books and articles which required more than just a recital of personal opinions.

Was his head turned by his acceptance into the world of New York financiers, by the red carpet treatment meted out by hopeful supplicants of aid, deference displayed by men of substance, by his success as a writer and speaker? This heady brew quite possibly was balanced by the calumny, anger, and obloquy he occasionally stirred up by taking unpopular stands on controversial issues.

Haygood was democratic and Jeffersonian. He believed in a society of honest yeomen engaged in agricultural pursuits, without large cities, heavy industry, banks, or other large institutions common to large, advanced industrial societies. The Methodist Episcopal Church, South, was about the largest private institution with which he had first-hand contact. The Slater trustees, Jesup, Stewart, and Dodge, on the finance committee, on the other hand, were at home with business, industry, banks, and cities. They knew and relied upon large Hamiltonian institutions, both public and private. They were not so far removed from the amassing of great American fortunes to have lost sight of the roles played by connections, guile, bribery, and ruthless ambition in human relations. Thus there was plenty of room for disagreement between Haygood and Jesup & Company even without Haygood's independence and decidedly untoady-like manner toward them.

Although Haygood was not entirely unfamiliar with the personal favor that can accrue to one who stands in well with men and women of influence, his own rapid rise in the church being due in no small part to his close personal ties to his church's senior bishop, George Pierce, he was at no pains to cultivate the most affluent Slater trustees, even though his own financial difficulties might have suggested this as the most prudent course of action for him. When he sought a personal loan (1889), he turned to Hayes, who was least able to grant it, although earlier (1885) he had sought funds for Emory College from the New York trustees. By 1889, he and the New Yorkers were increasingly alienated.

The Slater Fund's original resources consisted of $520,750 in railroad bonds and the balance of $1 million in cash.[14] The trustees continued to buy and sell railroad bonds in varying amounts (see appendix A). At the end of 1883, they had $955,000 invested in such securities. The following year, they purchased $170,000 and sold $74,685 in railroad bonds. In 1887 they purchased for the first time United States four percent bonds in the amount of $12,806. In the next two years, they purchased "U. S. Fours" in the amounts of $12,563 and $12,800. About ninety percent of their investments paid 6 percent interest with the balance about evenly divided between 5 and 4 percent bonds in the 1883-1891 period. Income from investments averaged over $61,500 annually; expenses averaged about $6,200.

The fund was worth $1,189,000 at the end of 1891 and reached $1.5 million in 1900. The only additions to the fund other than that resulting from investment income were gifts of $2,000 and $1,025,

[14] "Organization of the Trustees," p. 16.

given without conditions, by Smith Hirst of Flushing, Ohio. The gifts were given through Hayes, Hirst's friend. Hirst also gave through the Slater trustees $1,000 to the Slater Training School in Knoxville, Tennessee, in 1886.[15]

The trustees were indeed fortunate not to lose any investments in a period of frequent financial panics when many individuals, corporations, and trusts were financially ruined. Hayes wrote to Jesup of his concern for the trust's investments in railroads. He looked for hard times to occur frequently during the lifetime of the Slater trust when at least three-fourths of the railroads would fail to pay interest on their bonds. He hoped that Slater money would buy bonds of the remaining fourth which would continue to pay.[16]

The following month, the finance committee authorized the sale of the fund's Marietta and Cleveland Railroad bonds at par and interest. In the financial panic of May 5-7, 1884, the Marietta and Cleveland failed, but the Slater funds suffered no losses.

There was wholesale speculation in rail securities in the early eighteen eighties. Prosperity had returned after a six year hiatus following the financial panic of 1873. Many new rail issues appeared on the market and there was a fresh impetus to constructing new lines and extending others. Railway mileage increased by 7,000, 10,000, and 11,000 miles in 1880, 1881, and 1882 respectively. Railroads became overcapitalized, providing inducement for internal mismanagement. Huge stock returns were paid. In 1880, the Louisville & Nashville and the Chicago & Rock Island railroads each declared 100 percent dividends. Forty million dollars in dividends were paid to railroad shareholders in that year. By 1883, the economy was slowing down, and rail earnings dipped markedly. Eighteen eighty four brought another financial panic. The Metropolitan Bank in New York City, whose president, George I. Seney, was an Emory College benefactor, closed its doors as a result of a run. Seney was deep in speculative rail stock.

Railway mismanagement was revealed in statistics of receivership. In 1886, one hundred eight roads with track mileage of 11,000 were in the hands of receivers. Rail stock averages, up to 116 in 1882, dropped to 75 in 1885. Public demand to control railroads was aroused to the extent of eliminating such practices as discriminatory

[15] R. B. Hayes to M. K. Jesup, November 17, 1886, and R. B. Hayes to D. C. Gilman, January 20, 1887, Hayes MSS.. Rubin, *Teach the Freeman*, Vol. I, p. 185; vol. II, p. 35.

[16] R. B. Hayes to M. K. Jesup, November 23, 1882, Hayes MSS..

freight rates, rebates, drawbacks, and pooling of traffic. In February 1887, the Interstate Commerce Act became law. It required carriers to make tariffs public, standardize their accounting, and cease their most abusive practices.[17]

The Slater trustees must have had the most astute intelligence (Jesup was expert in railroad investments) together with a remarkable degree of good luck to have avoided losses from their railroad bonds during the early years of the fund.

The earliest direction of the operations of the Slater Fund was determined by the following critical conditions and events:

1. Instructions of the founder to the trustees relative to the objects he wished pursued: Education of blacks in the southern states, education to be leavened with a morality pursuant to Christian precepts; emphasis to be placed upon training black teachers, the whole effort aimed at helping the poor. The original trustees were conscious of these strictures as their successors have been over the last one hundred years. Even taking into account the changes in program emphases initiated by the Southern Education Foundation, one can still see these directions guiding the work of the Slater Fund successor. Without these injunctions, the Slater work and that of the SEF could be measurably different. See chapter eight for a discussion of the work of the Southern Education Foundation.

2. Appointment of (a) an agent, Haygood, who would vigorously pursue the goals of the founder, rather than an agent who might have been simply a friend or lackey of the founder or one or more of the original trustees, and (b) trustees who were equally committed to the cause. The leadership of the agent and original trustees is manifest in the accompanying narratives describing their efforts in behalf of black education in the South. The leading trustees, men like Hayes, Jesup, and Gilman, were as essential to the success of the Slater work as was Haygood. They set high standards for their successors when they made sure that the founder's work did not drift or stagnate. Few other foundations have been as fortunate in the selection of their leadership as was the Slater Fund.

3. The decision of the trustees to aid schools offering manual, as well as mental and moral, intruction.[18] When this decision was made,

[17] See Ida M. Tarbell, *The Nationalizing of Business: 1878-1898,* Vol. IX of *A History of American Life* (New York: MacMillan, 1936), pp. 91-103.

[18] Recent critics have raised the complaint that Slater Fund leaders did not seek to train a black industrial leadership, to train blacks to assume a leadership role in modernized industries. The Slater trust sponsored simple vocational training,

there were only a few black schools which actually offered manual instruction. When Haygood left the agency in 1891, every Slater-aided school offered such instruction. Despite the repudiation of industrial education by black leaders in this century, the popularization of industrial education by the Slater emphasis thereon was a powerful influence resulting in the establishment of state vocational colleges for blacks in all but three southern states. The three, Mississippi in 1871 and Virginia and South Carolina the following year, had already started such schools.

4. Haygood's open mind relative to the educability of blacks. He did not believe that blacks were racially inferior. If he had, the fund's efforts might have been subverted to become a convenience to the rich or to discourage rather than promote effort and self-reliance on the part of beneficiaries of the fund. The fund's helping hand, if extended with marked condescension, an emanation of racial superiority, would have likely contained a strong element of self-interest not conducive to the interests of recipients.

5. Appointment of investment experts to the board, especially Jesup, who saw to it that the fund's capital was not impaired but instead was increased through a policy of reinvestment of income. This was pursuant to Slater's instructions to the original trustees. But there was nothing automatic about the founder's desire being realized. Investment officers of public and private foundations face the same risks today. Few are as successful as Jesup and company were.

6. Haygood's failure to attend with regularity the meetings of the trustees to present his reports and answer questions relative to his views and grants was an administrative weakness which was corrected with the reorganization of the board in 1891 in which an education committee was established with a chairman, Curry, who in effect acted as agent for the trustees. Members of the board, strongly interested in being fully informed, were privy to the problem and corrected it, another indicator of just how well competent, interested officers made the Slater effort successful.

Based upon the experience of the original Slater board and logical extrapolations of its experience, one may posit certain critical aspects of foundation boards engaged in similar tasks as follows:

manual skills which are perceived to be more important in teaching morality and social conformity than in producing skilled artisans and leaders. See Roy Eugene Finkenbine, "A Little Circle: White Philanthropists and Black Industrial Education in the Postbellum South" (Unpublished Ph. D. Dissertation: Bowling Green State University, 1982), p. 3.

1. Employment of full-time qualified staff members who see intrinsic value in their work.

2. Make available to trustees and staff comprehensive and specific information relative to needs within the field of interests and objectives encompassed by the fundation's charter.

3. Systematically gather reliable feedback relative to results obtained from grants made or programs administered.

4. When appropriate, make effort to educate potential recipients of grants or beneficiaries of programs of the reasons for the board's initiatives.

5. When appropriate, make effort to educate targeted constituencies or the general public as needed regarding the foundation's initiatives, aims, and objectives.

6. Select trustees who have a focused interest in making the foundation successful in realizing its goals.

7. Maintain flexibility to change goals when circumstances indicate that change is essential or desirable.

8. Willingness of board members to establish responsibilities and procedures in bylaws or other directives media to the end of expediting efficient and effective administration.

9. Select trustees who together are representative of whatever geographical, vocational, avocational, racial, sexual, etc., factors are essential to the success of the trust's interests.

10. Award grants and administer programs so that recipients or beneficiaries are aware that aid to them is delivered on the self-help principle.

11. Efficient management of the financial resources committed to the care of the trustees.

12. Trustees to maintain effective oversight of the foundation's staff and its work.

13. Meetings of trustees held often enough and with sufficient preparation to avoid drift and stagnation in the foundation's operations and direction.

14. Adoption of standards or guides in the awarding of grants or the undertaking of program initiatives.

15. Insure that trustees know the bases for policy decisions and are consulted relative to proposed changes in policy.

16. Duties of trustees should involve trustees in meaningful and significant engagement so as to represent a challenge to each trustee.

17. Cultivate an honest and trusting relationship with staff members, beneficiaries, and other recipients of foundation appropriations as well as constituent groups and the public.

18. Trustees should concentrate their efforts on matters of policy and overall guidance of the foundation's efforts insofar as possible and permit staff members to have sufficient discretion to make decisions to commit the foundation to specific actions requiring knowledge of detailed information.

19. Compensate trustees and staff based upon a reasonable assessment of the value of the service rendered.

20. Insure that criteria used by the staff and trustees to evaluate the effectiveness of grants and programs are consistent with the basic goals and objectives of the trust.

In his final report as Slater agent, Haygood affirmed his commitment to the work of the Slater Fund and speculated about the results achieved. Statistics cannot adequately tell the story, he declared. Work done "for God's cause" cannot be expressed in numbers "as the 'Exchange' counts a cotton crop. 'Percentages' and 'averages' and 'totals' are inadequate in estimating efforts and results in the Spiritual Kingdom." He believed the results could only be accounted for in the future.

He was hopeful. He believed the "American-African race problem" would be solved. No one openly opposes educating blacks now, he asserted hopefully. But "a whole race cannot be educated in one generation." To those impatient to change the character of blacks, Haygood, the moralist, said that it was easier to learn arithmetic than to learn to speak the truth, to learn to read than to be honest; to learn science than to practice the industries, economics, and moralities of life; to learn books than to be manly. Haygood asserted that the current need of blacks was not a "regulation college curriculum." While he "would exclude, by arbitrary and proscriptive rules, no Negro from whatever he can achieve," since work opportunities for Negroes are limited "outside the labor of his hands," Slater aid rightfully emphasized industrial training. Those who need a college curriculum, he thought, were clergymen, teachers, and physicians. He believed that an hour or two a day in the work shop or serving room does not hinder in the least education in books. On the contrary, it fosters discipline and the development of personal character.

Haygood, much less the Slater trustees, was not crusading for civil rights for blacks. Haygood asserted that helping the black race "means bringing him to stand on his own feet, so that he will, by and by, need help no more." He believed that training and supplementary aid for Negroes must continue "for a hundred years to come—a very short time for so great a work."[19]

Of his role in the effort, Haygood wrote to Hayes of the shortness of the fight and the greatness of the work. It appeared to him that the better part of his life had passed since October 1882 when he first undertook the Slater agency.[20]

At the Slater board meeting in May 1891, a statement was entered into the minutes of the procedures which noted Haygood's retirement "in consequence of other responsible duties that he has assumed," and gave "grateful acknowledgements . . . for the careful review that he has made of the past nine years, and for the earnestness, devotion, and ability with which he has labored during all this period to carry out the purposes of this trust." The board noted "the very general interest that has been awakened . . . in the purposes of this trust . . ." and attributed this "in no slight degree" to Haygood's "good judgment . . . wise influence, and . . . acquaintance with all conditions of the problem. . . ."[21] Thus an era passed in the operation of the fund.

[19] The Slater Trustees *Proceedings* (1891), pp. 7-27, 28-39.
[20] A. G. Haygood to R. B. Hayes, September 18, 1890, Hayes MSS..
[21] The Slater Trustees *Proceedings* (1891), pp. 7-8.

# Chapter 8

# Is the Slater Model Applicable Today?

Within limitations set by the founder and trustees, Slater Fund efforts may be understood as a form of affirmative action taken to provide equal opportunity for blacks and to remedy past and current practices and the effects of racial discrimination.

The absence of large numbers of blacks in the professions and business in the early years of the Slater Fund was due to a long period of legally-sanctioned bondage followed by invidious discrimination which produced a lack of supply, that is, blacks who were qualified in terms of skills, knowledge, capital, and contacts to successfully operate in business and professional pursuits.

The Slater Fund brought to bear capital and directed effort which produced graduates with skills and knowledge. But the influence of the fund was little felt in generating either requisite capital or access thereto by impoverished blacks. Nor could the efforts of the fund produce the sort of contacts which have worked to produce successful careers for favored people.

Nevertheless, in a limited and rudimentary way, the Fund sought to redress an inequity of training and education which its successor trust, the Southern Education Foundation, continues.

The latter has gone forward, however, to give priority to efforts to insure equity in the desegregation of higher education and to address public policy issues relative to discrimination in public schools, two not unexpected emphases in the decades following the *Brown v. Board of Education* decision.

Thus in terms of affirmative action to help blacks to help themselves educationally, Slater Fund emphases which addressed the black situation a hundred years ago have been replaced. While no effort was made by Slater trustees in the 1880's and 1890's to attack and undo the legal, social, and vocational inequities which burdened blacks, the trustees attempted through changing the mental, behavioral, and vocational skills of blacks, as well as public perceptions thereof, to fit blacks for the sort of relatively free and unfettered citizenship to which Americans with no previous condition of servitude were accustomed.

The latter observation may be disputed by individuals who see a disquieting inconsistency in the Slater trustees' presumably noble concern for educating blacks whilst acquiescing in the States' and federal courts' stripping blacks of civil liberties. And some critics read ulterior motives into the trustees' insistence upon funding industrial education for blacks, an emphasis which is said to arise from a desire by business interests to make of blacks a large source of cheap and docile labor. These criticisms are addressed in chapter nine.

The Slater trustees acted pursuant to the will of the founder who hoped that the trust which he established would aid the freedmen to be "good men and good citizens." Slater wanted his trust to accomplish this through instruction "in the common branches of secular learning . . . [and] training in just notions of duty toward God and man, in the light of the Holy Scriptures."[1] The trustees added the emphasis on vocational skills which they felt would best carry out Slater's desires.

While there is no reason a late twentieth century educational trust could not continue an emphasis upon "conferring . . . [upon blacks], the blessings of Christian education," and to do so because of the "disabilities formerly suffered by these people,"[2] the successor to the Slater trust, the Southern Education Foundation, has changed its emphasis largely to one of helping blacks to attain the blessings of legal, social, and vocational equality.

The most recent *Annual Report* of the Southern Education Foundation states that: "Consonant with the interest of the donors, the Foundation continues to have as its principal purpose the advancement of equal and quality educational opportunity for Blacks in Southern states. SEF supports projects for children and youth, community groups, policy studies, colleges serving Blacks, local and regional desegregation programs, and some projects operated by the Foundation."

While requests for grants and their perceived need continue to

[1] See "Letter of the Founder," Appendix H.

[2] *Ibid.*.

rise, the foundation's operating programs require an increasing proportion of SEF activities.

The foundation no longer operates only from income produced by the four funds which derive from the initial donors. It serves as a conduit for funds from a variety of public and private sources to support the foundation's operating programs.

Administration of the Southern Education Foundation has departed from the spartan organization and staff of the incipient Slater Fund. The foundation's 1983-1984 *Annual Report* lists a staff of five headed by a president who also serves as a member of the board of directors. There are twelve directors, two consultants, and an advisory board of twenty. Blacks have moved into positions of leadership. Women serve as directors, advisors, and members of the permanent staff.[3]

The four funds which the foundation administers together with the balance of each at the end of the year ended March 31, 1984, are as follows:

| | |
|---|---|
| John F. Slater Fund | $4,700,710 |
| George Peabody Fund | 907,324 |
| Anna T. Jeanes Fund | 908,022 |
| Virginia Randolph Fund | 20,000 |
| TOTAL | $6,536,056[4] |

Among the foundation's operating programs there is, to take one as an example, a Higher Education Program which is funded as follows:

| | |
|---|---|
| SEF | $ 61,500 |
| Ford Foundation grant to SEF | 191,200[5] |

The SEF operates an Expanded Public Policy Program which had authorized funding of $316,455 in fiscal year 1984 which came from grants to SEF from the Ford Foundation, Lilly Endowment, the Rockefeller Foundation, and Carnegie Corporation of New York.[6]

In fiscal year 1984, the foundation authorized funding of grants in the amount of $363,246, while it authorized funding of operating programs in the amount of $835,122, a total of $1,198,368.[7]

Board chairman, Lisle C. Carter, Jr. voiced a foreboding that current federal policies may result in a denial of equal educational

[3] Southern Education Foundation, *1983-84 Annual Report,* p. 2.
[4] *Ibid.,* p. 19.
[5] *Ibid.,* p. 21.
[6] *Ibid.*.
[7] *Ibid.*.

opportunities. The directors accordingly set a theme for SEF to rededicate its resources to the realization of equality in education in the South within the limits of SEF's grants and operating programs.[8]

Foundation president Elridge W. McMillan announced that, with respect to grants, SEF would emphasize higher education, especially with respect to black colleges. With respect to elementary and secondary education, SEF would emphasize issue resolution rather than delivery of services. The Foundation will set a limit of $30,000 on any grant for a year and will continue to support specific activities rather than awarding grants for general support. High priority will go to continuing the foundation's efforts in focusing on the definition and resolution of Public Policy issues and in serving as broker and convenor of individuals around such issues. Likewise priority will be given to SEF's continuing efforts to insure equity in the desegregation of higher education. McMillan hopes SEF will stimulate the interest of other larger foundations in SEF's efforts.[9]

SEF's securities portfolio ranges far afield from the railroad and government bonds that were held in the 1880's and 1890's by the Slater trust. Although SEF held bonds (both government and corporate) with a market value slightly in excess of $2.5 million at the end of fiscal year 1984, the foundation held a broad assortment of common stocks representing 38 corporations with a market value of just under $4.8 million and preferred stock of two corporations valued at $0.294 million.[10]

Grants and programs of the foundation were categorized as:

1. Early Childhood Education, the largest grant ($25,000) of which went to support efforts by the Federation of Child Care Centers of Alabama, Inc. (FOCAL) of Montgomery to assist day care providers serving low income families in Alabama.

2. Undergraduate Education, the largest grant ($15,000) of which went to the University of South Carolina in Columbia for support of the "American South Comes of Age," an instructional telecourse on the Southern experience over the last quarter century.

3. Graduate and Professional Education, a category in which $20,000 was granted for support of the Summer Science-Engineering-Mathematics Institute conducted by Atlanta University's Resource Center for Science and Engineering.

[8] *Ibid.,* p. 3.
[9] *Ibid.,* pp. 4-5.
[10] *Ibid,* pp. 23-26.

4. Grants related to the SEF-Operated Higher Education Program, the largest grant ($6,500) of which went to Tennesseans for Justice in Higher Education in Nashville for support of advocacy and monitoring activities relative to desegregation of public higher education in Tennessee. Efforts in this category were aided by a grant from the Ford Foundation for support of research, monitoring, and technical assistance in the desegregation of higher education.

5. Grants Related to the SEF-Operated Public Policy Program, the largest grant ($50,000) of which went to the Southeastern Public Education Program of Macon, Georgia, for support of the programs' efforts to address issues such as parent involvement, students' rights and responsibilities, testing and test use, and areas related to discrimination in public schools.

6. SEF-Sponsored Activities, a category represented by two projects, one, the larger, consisting of a grant of $33,000 for sponsorship of a conference held in October 1983 titled: "Education in a Changing South: New Policies, Patterns and Programs." The conference support was provided in part by grants from the Ford Foundation and the Lilly Endowment.

7. Atlanta Community Support, a category outside SEF's normal grants program consisting of 25 grants usually of a few hundred dollars the largest of which ($3,500) went to the Atlanta Urban League.

8. General Contributions, a category of an unspecified number of grants most of which were grants of $200 and under, but the largest of which ($5,000) went to Hayes Mizell of Columbia, South Carolina, in a grant described as a contract for completion of a chapter of a book, *A New Education Agenda for the South.*

9. Miscellaneous, a category consisting of two grants of $3,000 each, one of which went to the Atlanta University Center to help defray expenses of a delegation of black scientists' visit to China for the purpose of scientific discourse and exchange. The second grant went to the Atlanta branch of the National Association for the Advancement of Colored People for support of a project to develop models and strategies for the purpose of increasing the number of minorities doing business with the Georgia Power Company.[11]

SEF is administering both investment income and grant money from other foundations. The mix occasioned the foundation to elect

[11] *Ibid.,* pp. 6-15.

to begin, effective April 1, 1983, a 60-month period required by statute to terminate its status as a private foundation and to become a public charity. The Federal Tax Code provides that if a private foundation receives more than one-third of its annual support from members and the general public and not more than one-third of its annual support from investment income, it no longer qualifies as a private foundation. It becomes a public foundation or public charity.[12] SEF's support varies, of course, from year to year in terms of proportions as well as amounts. But the foundation's experience determined the decision to seek public charity status.

SEF focuses vastly more on the issue of equity in education in the South than the early Slater trustees ever thought of. Of course, the educational scene has changed dramatically in the last one hundred years. A century ago financial support simply to keep schools for blacks open was a critical need. Since *Brown v. Board of Education* in 1954 and the resultant struggle to desegregate schools, insuring equity in desegregation plans and quality education have become paramount. Nor are SEF directors concerned so much for vocational and moral training as were the original Slater trustees.

The last hundred years have seen both change and continuity but not enough of the former nor so little of the latter that the trustees ever determined that there was no further serious need for the fund in the form that it was first instituted. The founder provided that in such a case, the trustees were authorized to apply the capital of the fund to "the establishment of foundations subsidiary to the already existing institutions of higher learning, in such wise as to make the educational advantages of such institutions more freely accessible to poor students of the colored race."[13]

The trustees of the Peabody Education Fund reached such a decision about their trust which was dissolved in 1914 and its assets divided three ways. But the assets of the Slater Fund, including the portion it received from the division of Peabody assets, went unencumbered into its successor trust, the Southern Education Foundation, in 1937.

[12] *Federal Tax Guide, 1985* (Chicago: Commerce Clearing House, 1984), p. 1,515 [¶ 4527A]. Practices which led the management of SEF to seek a change in the trust's status as a private foundation are of long standing. The Slater Fund was administering grants from larger foundations in support of Negro education prior to its merger into the Southern Education Foundation in 1937. See Ernest Victor Hollis, *Philanthropic Foundations and Higher Education* (New York: Columbia University Press, 1938), p. 48.

[13] "Letter of the Founder," Appendix H.

The Slater model continues to function in terms of a broad interpretation of the aims of the trust set up by its founder as well as in terms of some of the organizational and management practices of the founding trustees which were reviewed in the introduction and chapter seven. Changes in emphasis from teacher and industrial education to equity, trust-operated programs, and adjustments in funding made pursuant to the availability of or, alternately, the withholding of public funds are made within the same basic framework established by John F. Slater to which succeeding boards of trust have made adjustments.

Slater Fund assets made up 71.9 percent of the assets of the Southern Education Foundation at the end of fiscal year 1984. There is far more diversification in asset investment now than a hundred years ago. SEF assets are about six times the assets available to the Slater Fund in the 1882-1891 period. But the model still largely holds. It continues to be used as perhaps the oldest affirmative action program for blacks, other than the oldest traditionally black schools, in America.

# Chapter 9

# The Slater Model and Black Expectations

Two questions raised in chapter 8 need to be addressed at some length. Were the Slater trustees, and their agent, Haygood, inconsistent in showing concern for helping blacks educationally while appearing to be indifferent to the civil liberties of blacks? Or is the apparent inconsistency explained by the Slater principals simply being the tools of business interests who pushed blacks into industrial training in order to create a large body of cheap, docile labor to be exploited by business men both North and South?

Donald Spivey wrote that industrial training was a major force in the subjugation of black labor in the New South. Spivey characterized Samuel Chapman Andrews, founder of Hampton Institute, as the ideological father of black industrial education. Spivey wrote that Andrews believed that blacks should be taught to remain in their place, stay out of politics, keep quiet about their rights as citizens, and work steadily, subserviently, and uncomplainingly.[1]

Ronald E. Butchart wrote critically of Northern educational societies which, he said, wished blacks to respect property rights, acquiesce in the appropriation of surplus value, and accept exploitation and subordination. To the extent that blacks did these things, individuals connected with the societies characterized blacks as intelligent and possessed of good character. Conversely they were said to be ignorant and depraved.[2]

While freedmen sought education provided through whatever

[1] Donald Spivey, *Schooling for the New Slavery: Black Industrial Education, 1868-1915* (Westport, CT: Greenwood Press, 1978), pp. ix, x. Hereinafter cited as Spivey, *The New Slavery.*

[2] Ronald E. Butchart, *Northern Schools, Southern Blacks, and Reconstruction: Freedman's Education, 1862-1875* (Westport, CT: Greenwood Press, 1980), p. 60.

public or private agencies offered monetary or applied assistance, their greatest need, according to Butchart, was for land, justice, protection, and power. But educational agencies were largely silent on non-educational needs.[3]

Furthermore they were acquiescent on the issue of separate and unequal schools. William Preston Vaughn wrote that Barnas Sears, first agent of the Peabody Education Fund (1868-1880) adamantly opposed giving Peabody aid to integrated schools. Sears reasoned that since the majority of white Southerners vehemently opposed integrated schooling, aid to schools which were not racially segregated was harmful to the future prospects for public schools in the South.[4]

In 1874 Sears became involved in the shaping of Charles Sumner's Civil Rights Bill pending in Congress which, as originally drafted, had a clause which would have made integrated schools the norm. Sears felt the clause would undo the Peabody work unless the Sumner bill were "followed by another [law] requiring each state to maintain public schools of a given character, and still another requiring the attendance of white children."[5]

According to Vaughn, the Peabody board, which in 1874 included Chief Justice Waite, appointed that year and later of the Slater board, gave overwhelming approval to Sears' efforts opposing mixed schools and fighting for removal of the school clause from the Civil Rights Bill. They also approved the trust's aiding black schools during the Sears era according to a reduced scale of payments, which was two-thirds of the rates for white schools based upon school enrollment.[6]

With respect to opposition to mixed schools, however, Curry disagrees with Vaughn, writing in 1898 that the trustees and agent of the Peabody Fund were interested in encouraging a state interest in public schools which were new to the South. The Peabody managers were neutral on the issue of segregated versus racially mixed schools. They supported them whichever way local authorities set them up, according to Curry.[7]

What was the record of the first Slater Board President, Rutherford Hayes, toward blacks? As early as 1849, Hayes, in a

[3] *Ibid.*, p. 177.

[4] William Preston Vaughn, *Schools for All: The Blacks & Public Education in the South, 1865-1877* (Lexington: University of Kentucky Press, 1974), p. 153.

[5] *Ibid.*.

[6] *Ibid.*, p. 145.

[7] J. L. M. Curry, "A Brief Sketch of George Peabody," Peabody Education Fund (1898), p. 41.

diary entry, made clear his reservations about slavery while visiting his former classmate, Guy Bryan, in Texas.[8] As a Member of Congress in 1865, Hayes supported suffrage for the freedmen, but with an educational test.[9] Hardly one percent of blacks could read at that time. He approved passage of the Civil Rights Act of 1866.[10] In a diary entry on May 15, 1866, he wrote: "My decided preference: Suffrage for *all* in the South, colored and white, to depend on education . . . all *new* voters to be able to write and read."[11]

While travelling from Washington to New Orleans in December 1866, Hayes wrote his uncle, Sardis Birchard, from Memphis: "We meet the leading Rebels everywhere [He had been in Knoxville, Chattanooga, and Nashville]. The Rebel officers are particularly interesting. I get on with them famously. I talk negro suffrage and our extremest radicalism to all of them. They dissent but are polite and cordial."[12]

Again writing on black suffrage in a letter to his friend, Guy Bryan, in Galveston, November 23, 1876, Hayes wrote that he believed "(I hope I am mistaken) that Southern Democrats think it was a monstrous wrong to give the colored people the ballot, and that it is excusable in them if they, the Southern Democrats, in effect nullify the provisions of the Constitution which secure this right to colored men."[13]

In reviewing the compromise recently entered into to settle the election dispute and his accession to the Presidency in 1877, Hayes renewed his hopes for what blacks would get out of the settlement: ". . . The troops are ordered away, and I now hope for peace, and what is equally important, security and prosperity for the colored people. The result of my plan is to get from those States by their governors, legislatures, press, and people pledges that the Thirteenth, Fourteenth, and Fifteenth Amendments shall be faithfully observed, that the colored people shall have equal rights to labor, education, and the privileges of citizenship. I am confident this is a good work. Time will tell."[14]

While Hayes' confidence turned out to be misplaced, his good

[8] Williams, *Hayes' Diary and Letters,* Vol. I, p. 255.

[9] See diary entry for December 1, 1865, recounting a meeting of the Ohio Congressional delegation that evening. *Ibid.,* Vol. III, p. 7.

[10] R. B. Hayes to Lucy Hayes [wife], April 8, 1866. *Ibid.,* p. 22.

[11] Diary entry, May 15, 1866. *Ibid.,* p. 25.

[12] R. B. Hayes to S. Birchard, December 26, 1866. *Ibid.,* p. 37.

[13] *Ibid.,* p. 380.

[14] *Ibid.,* p. 430.

intentions were manifest. A few days later, he tried to implement his views in a letter to John E. King, United States Collector in New Orleans on May 7, 1877, by endorsing the employment of blacks by King in his office in positions for which they qualify and saying it "will tend to secure to people of their race consideration and will diminish race prejudice."[15]

Returning to a consideration of the compromise of 1877, Hayes wrote in his diary on April 11, 1880: "My task was to wipe out the color line, to abolish sectionalism, to end the war and bring peace." He observed that the war had not ended for many Southerners as long as their country was occupied.[16]

Hayes first began discussing favorably industrial education for blacks in 1882 in response to plans being laid for the Slater trust. He was not, however, unaware of industrial education since his son, Rutherford, was attending the Polytechnic Institute in Boston in 1881.[17]

In a diary entry for May 7, 1882, Hayes wrote of his hopes for blacks and of how he hoped the Slater Fund would help. "Industrial education, as well as religious education, must have attention. To make the colored people respected and influential, they must be successful in accumulating property—in doing the work which our civilization prizes most highly. Let them be not merely bookish scholars, but good mechanics and good business men. Let them show architects, civil engineers, and the like."[18]

Hayes believed in industrial training for all people. When Leland Stanford announced his plans to establish the university which bore the name of his son, Hayes wrote to Stanford rejoicing in his plans and the role that industrial education was to play in the university's curriculum. "Manual training," he wrote, "is fundamental. . . ."[19]

As to black rights, equality became increasingly insignificant as a national ideal with the passage of time after the Civil War. The Civil Rights Act of 1875 recognized the equality of all men before the law and gave blacks equal access to public accommodations. But the Act represented the high water mark of Radical Reconstruction. Thereafter the public in the North grew increasingly apathetic to vigorous enforcement of civil rights in the Southern states. Following

[15] *Ibid.*, p. 433.
[16] *Ibid.*, p. 595.
[17] R. B. Hayes to Fanny Rutherford Hayes [daughter]. *Ibid.*. Vol. IV, p. 40.
[18] *Ibid.*, p. 76.
[19] R. B. Hayes to Leland Stanford, December 12, 1885. *Ibid.*, p. 255.

the collapse of the remaining Radical Reconstruction governments in 1877 when federal troops were relieved of occupation duty, there emerged a federal predisposition to permit dominant southern whites in the states they controlled to determine the extent to which they would enforce constitutional guarantees of equal rights. Blacks were generally denied the right to vote, and Jim Crow determined that whites only had free access to public accommodations. Presidents who followed Grant, including Hayes, did nothing to interfere with the wishes of southern whites in their ordering of race relations. More pressing needs were seen to be national reunion and harmonious relations between the people of the states.[20]

Thus in the period when the Slater Fund began operations, it was easily perceived that it would be counter-productive for Slater Fund officials to insist upon racial equality for blacks when they wished to encourage white southerners to take up the task of providing educational opportunities for blacks. The opportunities, or so it was thought, would be segregated or not at all.

This view increasingly became the national view and was backed by a number of court decisions which gave the highest legal sanction to race as a basis for invidious distinctions between American citizens. Despite federal guarantees of rights imbedded in the Constitution, rights accorded to individuals because of their humanity, the courts went through a period of permitting states and local government to deny rights to blacks through laws that were not *prima facie* discriminatory. Thus the United States Supreme Court said that citizens had no right to vote, that states might proscribe voting by means of literacy tests, residency and registration reqirements, grandfather clauses, and poll taxes.

Chief Justice Waite, one of the original Slater trustees and a Peabody trustee as well, had a number of opportunities on the bench to strike a blow for justice for blacks. Louis Filler described Waite as anti-slavery but not pro-Negro. In these respects he was a typical Northern conservative. He opposed secession and armed resistance to federal authority. But he was anything but a Radical Republican in terms of being anti-Southern or pro-black.[21]

Waite's era on the court (1874-1888) was pro-states' rights. The

[20] *Freedom to the Free: A Report to the President by the United States Commission on Civil Rights* (Washington: Government Printing Office, 1963), pp. 45-56.

[21] Louis Filler, "Morrison R. Waite," *The Justices of the United States Supreme Court, 1789-1969: Their Lives and Major Opinions,* edited by Leon Friedman and Fred L. Israel, (New York: Chelsea House and R. R. Bowker Co., 1969), Vol. II, p. 1245.

*Slaughter House Cases* in 1873 set the legal tone of the Waite court the year before Waite's appointment, a court which was marked by a tolerance of state legislation in the economic field as well as indifference toward the rights of blacks. Waite played an important role in this development.[22]

Waite's decision in *United States v. Cruikshank* in 1874 indicated he had no desire to uphold Negro rights. In the case, white men in Louisiana had been arrested for breaking up a Negro political meeting and indicted under a section of the Congressional Enforcement Act of 1870 which prohibited interference with a person's federal rights. Waite's decision set them free since, he wrote, no federal right had been violated because the Fifteenth Amendment had not granted suffrage to Negroes.[23] The right to vote, according to Waite, came from the states.

In a succession of other cases, Waite acquiesced in wholesale assaults by the states on the rights of black citizens. In the case of *United States v. Reese* in 1876, the court voided part of the Enforcement Act of 1870 and severely qualified the Fifteenth Amendment. In *Neal v. Delaware* in 1880, Waite dissented from the majority saying that the mere exclusion of blacks from juries was not enough to demonstrate discrimination. In *Hall v. DeCuir* in 1878, he struck down for the court a Louisiana law requiring integration on carriers as a burden on interstate commerce. Waite concurred with the majority in the *Civil Rights Cases* in 1883, in which the court ruled on the question of nondiscrimination in admission to public accommodations, guaranteed in the Civil Rights Act of 1875. With only one dissent, that of Justice Harlan, a Hayes appointee, the court could find no constitutional warrant for the Civil Rights Act. Thus states could and did deny blacks public accommodations.[24]

Melville Fuller succeeded Waite both as Chief Justice and Slater trustee in 1888. The Fuller court (1888-1910) was characterized by Irving Schiffman as handing down a whole series of regressive decisions which permitted powerful ruling elements in America to hold back the free exercise of freedom by expanding constituencies. Fuller, a weak Chief Justice overshadowed by several other justices, was a supporting player in the court, but fully committed to the tenets of a conservative political supremacy.[25]

[22] *Ibid.*, p. 1249.
[23] *Ibid.*, pp. 1254-1255.
[24] *Ibid.*, p. 1255.
[25] Irving Schiffman, "Melville W. Fuller," *ibid.*, p. 1471.

As a states' rights, strict constructionist, and popular sovereignty Democrat in the 1850's, Fuller admitted to a belief that slavery was an evil. But he was equally opposed to secession and abolitionism. During the Civil War, Fuller proclaimed loyalty to the Union while denouncing the conduct of the war and staying out of uniform. The latter was a bone of contention in the hearings which preceded his confirmation by a less-than overwhelming vote as Chief Justice in 1888.[26]

Fuller voted with the majority of the court in the epochal case of *Plessy v. Ferguson* in 1896 affirming that states could segregate races on public conveyances. Within the next two decades, the states desiring to do so introduced racial segregation into just about any activity the mind of men could conceive—all modes of passenger transportation, eating places, drinking fountains, places of amusement, public parks, barber shops, juries, business offices, government agencies, marriage.

Another Slater trustee, J. L. M. Curry, has been accused of espousing views on education for blacks which would have blacks taught elementary industrial skills together with an acculturation which would act as social control insuring that blacks would accept the white man's values involving racial etiquette, discipline, and a predisposition to accept, acquiesce, and not ask questions about white leaders' plans for them.

Donald Spivey sees Curry as the master propagandist for these self-serving views. Spivey believes that Curry's advocacy of black education was simply a result of his having offered to prepare for Northern and Southern business interests a cheap and docile labor force in the form of the freedmen.[27]

In more than one of his publications issued by the Slater trustees, Curry projected a view of blacks and their abilities which was a sharp break from the views of the Slater Fund's first spokesman, Haygood. In 1895 Curry published an essay in which he expressed a race-consciousness and an estimate of the black race which was not flattering. While other races have made progress in bettering themselves and their institutions, Curry wrote, blacks have not. ". . . Whatever progress has marked . . . [the black's] life as a race in this country has come from without. The great ethical and political

[26] *Ibid.*, pp. 1473-1474.
[27] Spivey, *The New Slavery*, pp. 79-80, 84.

revolutions of enlightened nations through the efforts of succeeding generations, have not been seen in his history."

Curry believed that the greatest obstacle to educating blacks was found in the subjects themselves who by and large do not have the moral character, the "discipline of virtue," frugality or thrift, foresight, acquisitiveness, or ennobling home life to be much helped by northern efforts to aid them.

Curry even quoted two unnamed contemporaries who believed it would be beneficial to re-enslave blacks to teach them to work and to avoid "doing everything that God disapproves of." The latter doubtless would include everything proscribed by the tenets of middle class morality and religion of the time.

Curry believed that results produced by black colleges and universities had been mixed. He approved of denominational schools which offered industrial training. That is, he approved of combining moral, religious, and hand training. But he wrote that high schools and colleges for blacks which offered courses in the classics were misguided.

Curry concluded that educators should emphasize training in character and virtue, domestic, social, and home life, thrift, avoidance of waste, "of having a stake in good government," training in manual skills, reliance upon public schools, and harmony between the races in all communities.[28]

On the other hand, Curry's support of the Blair Bill for federal aid to education in 1884 indicated that he would not have insisted on segregated schooling. The Blair Bill would have desegregated schools. Of course, it is possible that Curry's views changed between 1888 and 1895 when he wrote so disapprovingly of limitations of blacks. White opinions of blacks generally became harsher in the 1890's.

The Slater board's treasurer, Morris K. Jesup, has been cited for attempting to subjugate blacks as a servile and docile work force for the enrichment of acquisitive business interests during the period of his trusteeship. Jesup had become a powerful figure in the railroad industry with significant pecuniary interests North and South by the end of the Civil War and was known as the leading investment broker in Southern railway bonds. We are told that there was a saying on Wall Street that "if it ran on two rails and was located in the

[28] J. L. M. Curry, "Difficulties, Complications, and Limitations Connected with the Education of the Negro," The Trustees of the John F. Slater Fund, *Occasional Papers*, No. 5 (1895), pp. 5, 14, 16-18, 19, 22-23.

South and you wanted to buy some stock in it, then Morris K. Jesup was the man to see."[29]

Other than Jesup's railroad and Wall Street connections, however, it is not quite clear what might lead one to believe that Jesup's motivations in aiding black education were anything but pure and unblemished. Nor have we a hint as to Jesup's conspiratorial connections with other powerful people who might want to make blacks into a large and willing source of cheap labor.

That acquisitive and unscrupulous people exist, and perhaps always have, who have a strong vested interest in hoaxing people into accepting their claims on them and having their way in terms of accountability, or a lack thereof, and wages, is indisputable. But with no more than slight circumstantial evidence implicating Jesup, or, for that matter, Curry, one must withhold judgment.

What then may be said about the Slater trustees, the founder, John F. Slater, and the agent, Atticus Haygood, with respect to their attitudes toward educating blacks, their emphasis on industrial education, their attitudes toward racial equality and civil rights for blacks? Neglect of the racial equality and civil rights issue for blacks following the Civil War and Reconstruction particularly by whites who lived outside the southern states, away from the great bulk of blacks, meant simply that blacks in the United States were to suffer an enforced peonage, a social and economic servitude for the better part of a century, the worst effects of which are still evident. Was this too great a price to pay for national amity, a condition enjoyed by the privileged? It was if you were one of the oppressed. It was in economic terms because of the loss of the most creative labor of blacks. Similarly it depressed the cultural and social contributions of blacks, thus diminishing the nation's output. Morally it was indefensible if one believes that such human repression is reprehensible.

Were southern whites less culpable in the oppression of blacks than whites outside the South? Of course, those southern whites who oppressed blacks because they employed them or competed with them and wished to do so with as little expense to themselves as possible were as culpable as anyone. But the great bulk of whites in the South acquiesced in the suppression of blacks because the mores indicated to them that it was normal for blacks to be unequal, poor,

[29] Spivey, *The New Slavery*, p. 72, quoting *Commercial and Financial Chronicle*, 10 (4 June 1870), p. 722.

subservient, relatively uneducated, with little or no capital, virtually invisible in business and the professions, and, of course, segregated. Only a small minority of southern whites could see unrealized potential in blacks. The mores can make anything right, and most people follow the mores without question.

There were southern whites who affected a belief in the uneducability of blacks. Indeed the alleged uneducability of blacks in the slave period justified the blacks' enforced labor. Conversely, however, masters believed, according to Charles S. Johnson, that education tended to make blacks less useful as laborers since education gave rise to discontent with social roles and doctrines as well as the threat of insurrection.

But slaveholders showed a lack of faith in their belief in the blacks' mental capacity by passing laws to prevent slaves from acquiring knowledge.[30] After emancipation, they sought still to encumber blacks from getting education by failing to provide public education for blacks as they did for whites. Why were efforts to deprive blacks of education undertaken?

After emancipation, the answer to the question lay in part in niggardliness, in an unwillingness to be taxed to pay for schools for black children. The Freedmen's Bureau and the northern missionary agencies expressed the idea that blacks possessed the same mental capacities as whites and that the blacks' *apparent* inferiority was due to the debasing effects of slavery.[31]

Similarly, Atticus Haygood, the Slater agent, declared that he did not know the relative capacity of the two races (white and black), but that schools should assist blacks in developing themselves to the limit of their abilities. Then and only then could the ability of blacks be measured.

In his book, *Our Brother in Black,* Haygood questioned the widespread assumption that blacks were inherently inferior to whites. "If anything in this world is settled," he wrote, "it is settled that the Negro can learn to read, to write, and to 'cipher.' And he learns well and rapidly."[32]

Others continued to oppose education for blacks who believed as

[30] Charles S. Johnson, *The Negro in American Civilization* (New York: Henry Holt, 1930), pp. 224-225. Hereinafter cited as Johnson, *The Negro.*

[31] D. O. W. Holmes, *The Evolution of the Negro College* (New York: Columbia University, 1934), pp. 68-69. Hereinafter cited as Holmes, *Negro College.*

[32] Atticus Haygood, *Our Brother in Black* (Nashville: Southern Methodist Publishing House, 1881), p. 134. Hereinafter cited as Haygood, *Our Brother.*

did John C. Calhoun that only if a Negro could be found who could give the syntax of a Greek verb would he be inclined to call him human.[33] But black students at schools such as Fisk University in Nashville were learning Greek syntax and more shortly after emancipation. Indeed, of the eighteen colleges of a philanthropic and missionary character established immediately preceding and following the Civil War, and the additional thirteen colleges founded by southern church organizations between 1870 and 1890, only Hampton and Tuskegee were not devoted almost exclusively to the old type of higher learning, the classics, theology, letters, and the humanities.[34]

D. O. W. Holmes wrote that the classical type of education was emphasized to a degree which was utterly inconsistent with the social pattern of recently freed slaves.[35] The pattern provided fuel for scoffers.

Further, southern white attitudes toward educating blacks were conditioned by the newness of the concept of universal education. Those who were most eager to get on with a workable program for educating blacks were those who had been won over to the idea that universal education was beneficial for people as well as the economy. J. L. M. Curry of the Slater board had been won over to the idea when he was a student at Harvard in 1844.

In most parts of the South, however, universal education was a novel idea in the years following the Civil War and was not embraced by all people by any means. Those who did *not* could be counted on to be either indifferent or antagonistic toward the idea of educating blacks. People with conservative biases could be counted on to oppose any education program which depended upon their tax contributions. Up to the 1860's in most parts of the South, such people had rather successfully opposed systems of comprehensive public schools for whites throughout the region.

Another key to southern white opposition to schools for blacks was the role of missionary teachers from the North who were perceived as teaching blacks to aspire to social equality with whites. Furthermore, during the Reconstruction period when the Freedmen's Bureau established schools for blacks all over the South, the Bureau worked closely with Radical politicians, and its control of the

[33] Johnson, *The Negro,* p. 224.
[34] John W. Davis, "The Negro Land-Grant College," *Journal of Negro Education,* 11 (July 1933), p. 314.
[35] Holmes, *Negro College,* p. 67.

schools was seen in both the North and South to involve control of the black vote.[36] Other southern whites opposed schools for blacks because they felt that education spoiled blacks as laborers without fitting them for anything else.

But the South did not speak with one voice on the subject. In 1903, during a period when black repression was at its height, Walter B. Hill, chancellor of the University of Georgia, counselled against those who said that the South could not afford to do justice to Negroes educationally since they believed that the result would be to disturb the social inequality that existed between the races by bringing Negroes into serious competition with whites. Hill declared: "I would say that the only thing which the South cannot afford in its relation to the Negro race is injustice."[37]

Some southern whites spoke contradictorily of rights for blacks seemingly without awareness of the contradiction. One of Haygood's critics wrote in a church paper in reply to Haygood's plea for equal opportunities for blacks so that they might realize their potential that he agreed that blacks should be given legal rights and that there were "thousands of men, just, patriotic, and pious" in the South who would see to the fair administration of justice to Negroes, but who also "will see to it that the supremacy of the white over the Negro race be maintained, and that the social separateness of the races be preserved. . . ." He deprecated any teaching or influence which tended to disquiet the Negro in his subordinate sphere and to stimulate in him an ambition not compatible with the supremacy of the white race. "Bottom rails there must be. . . . Let the distances between the races be maintained, and, if possible, increased." Concluding, he accused Haygood of immaturity and spoke of his "overwrought brain."[38]

George W. Cable, the Louisiana novelist whose unpopular racial views made him an exile in the North, wrote witheringly of the failure of southern whites to grant Negroes equal rights. He lashed out at segregationists, "adherents of the old regime . . . [who stood] in the way to every public privilege and place—steamer landing, railway platform, theater, concert-hall, art display, public library, public school, court house, church, everything—flourishing the

[36] H. L. Swint, *The Northern Teacher in the South, 1862-1870* (Nashville: Vanderbilt University Press, 1941), p. 142.

[37] Walter B. Hill, "Negro Education in the South," *Annals* of the American Academy of Political and Social Sciences, Vol. XXII (September 1903), p. 80.

[38] Nashville *Christian Advocate*, October 20, 1883.

hot branding iron of ignominious distinctions."[39]

Cable deplored the fact that the cornerstone of race relations in the South was inequality, that contact between members of the two races was countenanced as long as it was not on an equal footing. Cable stated that, although post-war whites in the South acknowledged that slave holding was wrong, they continued to hold blacks in servitude. And northerners acquiesced in the condition despite (as he saw it) winning the war to free the slaves, consoling themselves with the idea that at least winning the war had saved the Union! So now (he wrote in 1888), white northerners and southerners clasp each other in union of friendship while blacks are almost forgotten. Negroes were virtually subjects and peasants, not citizens! And the people of the South, black and white alike, with their segregated schooling, were missing the amalgamation of diverse populations afforded by the public school which had produced commercial skills and great wealth in the North. Cable averred that the South's inhospitality to universal education kept it poor and racially divided.[40]

Ruling white southerners had not followed the path to racial accommodation envisioned by the martyred President, Abraham Lincoln. While the War of the Rebellion was yet undecided, Lincoln sought the re-establishment of southern state governments by residents thereof who were loyal to the central government. In a letter to Major General N. P. Banks in Louisiana in August 1863, Lincoln expressed the hope that the people, in establishing a new state government, would adopt a system whereby whites and blacks "could gradually lift themselves out of their old relation to each other, and both come out better prepared for the new. Education for young blacks should be included in the plan." Lincoln did not object to temporary restrictions on the civil liberties of blacks so long as the new state government recognized the permanent nature of the blacks' freedom and took steps to prepare blacks for assuming the responsibilities of citizenship.

In March 1864 when Louisiana prepared to draw up a new state constitution, Lincoln wrote to Michael Hahn, the newly-elected governor, relative to the state convention and the question of who would be included in the electorate: "I barely suggest for your

[39] George W. Cable, "The Freedman's Case in Equity," *Century*, Vol. XXIX (January 1885), pp. 409-418.

[40] George W. Cable, "The Negro Question," The American Missionary Association (1888), pp. 1-32.

private consideration, whether some of the colored people may not be let in—as, for instance, the very intelligent, and especially those who have fought gallantly in our ranks. They will probably help in some trying time to come, to keep the jewel of liberty within the family of freedom."[41]

Doubtless with the best of intentions, Lincoln was willing to permit southern whites to work out the relationships of the races so long as progress was being made toward integration of blacks into the electorate, an eventuality which depended, as he saw it, upon education for blacks.

Lincoln's untimely death precluded his judgment upon whether the process of integration was too fast, too slow, or about right in the years following the war. Nevertheless, Lincoln's view of civil rights for blacks in the South seems to be remarkably similar to those of the Slater trustees whose expressions of opinion on the subject are available to us. Education was a precondition for unfettered exercise of civil liberties.

Might not the Slater trustees have been put off by the obvious animus shown by influential whites who, in Cable's words, stood in the blacks' way to every privilege, and who appeared determined never to permit racial equality to exist? Only Haygood, who was not a trustee, but their agent, expressed himself on this volatile issue. In his book, *Our Brother in Black,* in 1881, Haygood sought to induce southern whites to undertake the elevation of blacks and attacked the apprehensions of those who foresaw black domination looming ahead as a result of their education. "Do not . . . scare at this word 'elevation,'" he wrote. "Nothing is said about 'putting the Negro above the white man.' Let me whisper a secret in your ear: *That cannot be done unless you get below him.*"[42]

Social equality was a much feared theme to audiences of southern whites. Speakers who spoke up for blacks such as Haygood and Bishop Charles B. Galloway, a Slater trustee after the Haygood era, had to repeatedly reassure their audiences that there was no such thing as social equality in the natural order of things. Accordingly, their audiences should hear them out and not turn them out when they spoke on behalf of blacks.

Of course, the primary thrust of the Slater Fund, education (even industrial education) for blacks, would in due course of time

[41] Letters quoted in Benjamin P. Thomas, *Abraham Lincoln* (New York: Alfred A. Knopf, 1952), pp. 406-407.
[42] Haygood, *Our Brother,* p. 129.

inevitably pose a threat to the superior-inferior relationship of the races in the South. Educated blacks would reach a point where they would no longer be willing to remain subservient. Haygood, Galloway, and others like them must have known this. But they dared not reveal this to southern white audiences.

One of the means used by southern whites to reinforce the inferior status of blacks is found in inequalities in expenditures for white and black schools. Although the practice was of long duration, attention was first drawn to it in the Report on Negro Education of the United States Bureau of Education in 1916 by Thomas Jesse Jones. Jones reported that average per capita expenditures for education of whites in the southern states was $10.32 and of blacks, $2.89. The sociologist, Charles S. Johnson, believed from all available evidence that there was an obvious need for federal legislation to rectify the inequity of southern states, with the meagerest resources of any states, supporting dual school systems and doing so very badly.[43]

Another means of reinforcing black inferiority was to disfranchize blacks. Haygood had used the black as citizen and voter as an argument for educating blacks. The argument became less cogent as one by one the southern states took the vote from blacks.

For more than twenty years following the end of Reconstruction, blacks were disfranchized by intimidation and other overt measures not conformable with statutes. Gradually, beginning with Mississippi in 1890, the states enacted laws with the explicit purpose of eliminating blacks from politics. The laws accomplished their purpose by:

1. Tax test (poll or payment of all taxes owed six months before the election).
2. Property test (ownership of minimum amounts of real or personal property).
3. Educational test (read and write or read and write and/or interpret the state constitution).

Of course, election officials had discretionary powers in enforcing the tests in order to insure that deserving whites were not disfranchized.[44]

Was industrial training further intended to demean blacks and further reinforce their post-war servitude? Blacks in large numbers

[43] Johnson, *The Negro*, pp. 236, 265-266.
[44] *Ibid.*, pp. 338-340.

opposed the trend toward industrial training, a trend set in motion by the Slater Fund.[45] White interest in hand training was enough to turn many blacks against it. Later when most southern states established agricultural, mechanical, or industrial colleges for blacks (but no liberal arts, graduate, or professional schools), it seemed to many urban and small-town blacks that white patrons were primarily interested in the training of domestics.[46]

In the last years of the century, however, a decline set in in industrial training for blacks in schools calling themselves colleges. Industrial training flourished best in the state-sponsored land-grant colleges. But in most of the private schools, emphasis resumed on traditional higher learning. It became too expensive to support both industrial training and college work in these schools.[47]

Fisk University was an example of the latter, receiving Slater aid during the Haygood era but being dropped by 1895. Administrators and staff at Fisk, however, never lost sight of their aim to "establish among the colored youth the conviction of the absolute necessity of patient, long-continued, exact, and comprehensive work in preparation for high positions and large responsibilities. . . . [This is] fundamental to the accomplishment of the true mission of the University. Solid, radical and permanent results . . . [are] sought in all methods of work."[48]

Were the Slater principals inconsistent in their support of black expectations? Did they compromise here in order to gain an advantage there? Did their own aims and expectations for blacks blind them to the reality of how difficult it was going to be to help blacks to help themselves given the obstacles faced? I believe the answer to each of these questions is an affirmative one. Could they have done more than they did? Again the answer must be yes.

But to the question of whether the Slater principals were at bottom indifferent to black aims and expectations because they were simply errand-runners for unscrupulous exploitive interests, the answer must be no, insofar as the record goes. In terms of what we know of their careers, their interests, and their recorded thoughts, they appear to have been genuinely pursuing benevolent, philanthropic goals however imperfectly.

[45] Holmes, *Negro College,* p. 13.
[46] Johnson, *The Negro,* p. 296.
[47] Holmes, *The Negro College,* p. 152.
[48] "Catalogue of the Officers and Students of Fisk University, Nashville, Tennessee, for 1895-1896," (1896), p. 5.

Would they have refused to fund a school which offered a more ambitious program of industrial education including the training of industrial leaders and managers? Since they were dealing with a constituency which habitually operated on the sparest level of poverty, no school that we know of proposed such an ambitious program. If one had, there is nothing in the record to indicate that it would have been rejected out of hand by members of the Slater circle.

One may question the recorded thoughts of the two Chief Justices, Waite and Fuller, whose court opinions and concurrences largely mirrored the social and racial mores of the period. Anyone interested in progressive philanthropy would wish that they had been more of the mind and character of Justice John M. Harlan of Kentucky, their contemporary on the court who seemed to have a more sensitive and heightened grasp of the meaning of equal protection than his fellow justices had.

With respect to the original, most influential Slater principles, however, they appear to have been healthy-minded individuals who "did what they said and said what they did" without ulterior motives of a dark and sinister nature. Haygood was emphatically not another George W. Cable, a fellow Southerner whose outspokenness on racial equality made it unlikely that he could stay in the South with any degree of safety or serenity.[49] Nor was Hayes another Gilbert Haven, a fellow scion of New England whose unremitting efforts to abolish caste in America ended in apparent failure when he died in 1880.[50] But in their own ways, as they were able to concentrate and make felt their personal gifts and insights, the Slater principles appear to have been sincerely motivated with a sense of the public interest as well as personal, if not corporate, accountability which seems to be altogether rare in people even today, a hundred years later.

[49] See Arlin Turner, *George W. Cable, A Biography* (Baton Rouge: Louisiana State University Press, 1966).

[50] See William B. Gravely, *Gilbert Haven, Methodist Abolitionist: A Study in Race, Religion, and Reform, 1850-1880* (Nashville: Abingdon Press, 1973).

# APPENDICES

*Appendix A*

## SECURITIES (BONDS) BOUGHT AND SOLD

## JOHN F. SLATER FUND

## 1883-1891

| YEAR | BOUGHT | SOLD |
|---|---|---|
| 1883 | $955,000[1] | |
| 1884 | 170,000 | $74,685 |
| 1885[2] | | |
| 1886 | 50,710 | 45,573 |
| 1887 | 12,806[3] | |
| 1888 | 12,563[3] | 26,250 |
| | 25,083 | |
| 1889 | 85,330[3] | 65,445 |
| | 12,800[3] | |
| 1890 | 17,043 | 61,500 |
| 1891 | 70,588 | |

[1] Less $520,750 included in initial Slater bequest.
[2] Figures for 1885 not available.
[3] United States bonds (4 percent)

*Appendix B*

## INCOME AND ADMINISTRATIVE EXPENSES

## JOHN F. SLATER FUND

## 1883-1891

| YEAR | (a) INCOME[1] | (b) ADMINISTRATIVE EXPENSES[2] | (c) PERCENTAGE (b) ÷ (a) |
|---|---|---|---|
| 1883 | $ 62,632 | $ 3,436 | 5.5 |
| 1884 | 52,419 | 3,902 | 7.4 |
| 1885[3] | | | |
| 1886 | 58,750 | 6,774 | 11.5 |
| 1887 | 60,220 | 6,725 | 11.2 |
| 1888 | 63,707 | 6,718 | 10.5 |
| 1889 | 63,768 | 6,818 | 10.7 |
| 1890 | 64,690 | 6,709 | 10.4 |
| 1891 | 65,855 | 7,691 | 11.7 |
| TOTAL | $492,041 | $48,773 | |
| AVERAGE | 61,505 | 6,097 | 9.9 |

[1] From interest on bonds.

[2] Includes salary of general agent, lodging and traveling expenses of agent and trustees, clerical expenses of agent, secretary and treasurer of the board, cost of printing annual and special reports, stationery, postage.

[3] Figures for 1885 not available.

*Appendix C*

## OBJECTS OF DISBURSEMENTS

## JOHN F. SLATER FUND

## 1883-1891

| YEAR | Colleges & Universities | Hampton & Tuskegee | Private Secondary Schools | Public Schools | State Normal Schools | Direct Student Aid | TOTAL |
|---|---|---|---|---|---|---|---|
| 1883 | $ 11,000.00 | $ 2,100 | $ 2,700 | $ 450 | | | $ 16,250.00 |
| 1884 | 9,266.66 | 1,000 | 3,590 | | $ 2,700 | $ 550 | 17,106.60 |
| 1885 | 23,614.10 | 3,000 | 7,200 | 500 | 2,000 | 450 | 36,764.16 |
| 1886 | 17,300.00 | 3,900 | 6,350 | 500 | 1,500 | 450 | 30,000.00 |
| 1887 | 23,750.00 | 4,000 | 9,510 | 540 | 1,700 | 500 | 40,000.00 |
| 1888 | 26,510.00 | 4,000 | 11,090 | 1,000 | 1,900 | 500 | 45,000.00 |
| 1889 | 28,660.00 | 3,500 | 9,650 | 800 | 1,200 | 500 | 44,310.00 |
| 1890 | 27,660.00 | 3,500 | 9,250 | 800 | 1,200 | 500 | 42,910.00 |
| 1891 | 33,100.00 | 4,000 | 9,550 | 1,000 | 1,500 | 500 | 49,650.00 |
| TOTAL | $200,860.76 | $29,000 | $68,890 | $5,590 | $13,700 | $3,950 | $321,990.76 |

Source: Butler, "An Historical Account," pp. 111, 450.

## OFFICERS AND COMMITTEES

## THE SLATER TRUSTEES

**1882-1891**
**(Dates refer to year entered on duty)**

1. PRESIDENT
   R. B. Hayes (1882)

2. VICE PRESIDENT
   M. R. Waite (1882; died March 23, 1888)
   Melville W. Fuller (1891)

3. SECRETARY
   D. C. Gilman (1882)

4. TREASURER
   M. K. Jesup (1882)

5. EXECUTIVE COMMITTEE (established 1882)
   R. B. Hayes (1882)
   A. H. Colquitt (1882)
   W. E. Dodge, Sr. (1882; died February 9, 1883)
   J. P. Boyce (1882; died December 28, 1888)
   D. C. Gilman (1882)
   M. R. Waite (1883; replaced Dodge; died March 23, 1888)
   P. Brooks (1884; resigned January 5, 1889)
   H. C. Potter (1891)
   J. A. Broadus (1891)

6. FINANCE COMMITTEE (established 1882)
   J. A. Stewart (1882)
   W. E. Dodge, Sr. (1882; died February 9, 1883)
   M. R. Jesup (1882)
   W. E. Dodge, Jr. (1883; replaced Dodge, Sr.)

7. EDUCATION COMMITTEE (established 1890)
   J. L. M. Curry (1890)
   A. H. Colquitt (1890)
   J. A. Broadus (1890)
   R. B. Hayes (1890) *ex officio*
   D. C. Gilman (1890) *ex officio*
   M. R. Jesup (1890) *ex officio*

*Appendix E*

## ATTENDANCE AT SLATER BOARD MEETINGS

### 1882-1891

### Meetings by Years and Numbers

| | 1882 | | 1883 | | 1884 | 1885 | | 1886 | 1887 | 1888 | 1889 | | 1890 | | 1891 |
|---|---|---|---|---|---|---|---|---|---|---|---|---|---|---|---|
| TRUSTEES | 1 | 2 | 3 | 4 | 5 | 6 | 7 | 8 | 9 | 10 | 11 | 12 | 13 | 14 | 15 |
| Hayes | x | x | x | x | x | x | x | x | x | x | x | x | x | x | x |
| Waite[1] | x | x | | | x | | x | x | | | | | | | |
| Brooks[2] | | | | | | x | | | | | | | | | |
| Gilman | x | x | x | x | x | x | x | x | x | x | x | x | | x | x |
| Stewart | x | x | x | x | x | x | x | | x | x | x | x | | x | x |
| Colquitt | x | x | x | x | | x | | | x | x | | | x | x | x |
| Jesup | x | x | x | x | | x | x | x | | x | x | x | | x | x |
| Boyce[3] | x | x | x | x | x | x | | x | x | x | | | | | |
| Slater | x | x | x | x | x | x | | | x | x | x | x | | x | x |
| Dodge, Sr.[4] | | | | | | | | | | | | | | | |
| Dodge, Jr.[5] | | | | x | x | x | x | x | x | | x | x | x | x | x |
| Potter[6] | | | | | | | | | | | | x | | x | |
| Fuller[6] | | | | | | | | | | | | | | | |
| Broadus[7] | | | | | | | | | | | | | | x | x |
| Curry[8] | | | | | | | | | | | | | | | x |
| OTHERS (Non-trustees invited to meetings) | | | | | | | | | | | | | | | |
| Haygood | | | | x | x | | x | | x | x | | | x | | |
| Curry[8] | | | | | | | x | | | | | | | | |
| G. J. Orr[9] | | | | | | | x | | | | | | | | |
| W. H. Hickman[10] | | | | | | | | | | | | | x | | |

*Appendix E*

[1] Died after ninth meeting.
[2] Resignation accepted at eleventh meeting.
[3] Died after tenth meeting.
[4] Died after second meeting.
[5] Elected at third meeting.
[6] Elected at eleventh meeting.
[7] Elected at twelfth meeting.
[8] Elected at fourteenth meeting.
[9] Georgia State Superintendent of Schools.
[10] President of Clark University, Atlanta, Georgia.

*Appendix F*

**SLATER TRUSTEES**
**SHOWING THE STABILITY OF BOARD MEMBERSHIP**
**1882-1906**

| 1882 | 1886 | 1891 | 1896 | 1901 | 1906 |
|---|---|---|---|---|---|
| R. B. Hayes, *Pres.* | Hayes, *Pres.* | Hayes, *Pres.*[1] | | | |
| M. R. Waite, *VP.* | Waite, *VP.* | | | | |
| D. C. Gilman, *Sec.* | Gilman, *Sec.* | Gilman, *Sec.* | Gilman, *Pres.* | Gilman, *Pres.* | Gilman, *Pres.* |
| M. K. Jesup, *Trea.* | Jesup, *Trea.* | Jesup, *Trea.* | Jesup, *Trea.* | Jesup, *Trea.* | Jesup, *Trea.* |
| P. Brooks | Brooks | | | | |
| J. A. Stewart | Stewart | Stewart | Stewart | Stewart | Stewart |
| A. H. Colquitt | Colquitt | Colquitt[2] | | | |
| J. P. Boyce | Boyce | | | | |
| W. Slater | Slater | Slater | Slater | Slater | Slater |
| W. E. Dodge, Sr. | | | | | |
| | W. E. Dodge, Jr. | Dodge | Dodge | Dodge[3] | |
| | | M. W. Fuller, *VP.* | Fuller, *VP.* | Fuller, *VP.* | Fuller, *VP.* |
| | | H. C. Potter | Potter | Potter | Potter |
| | | J. A. Broadus[4] | | | |
| | | J. L. M. Curry | Curry, *Sec.* | Curry, *Sec.*[5] | |
| | | | W. J. Northen[6] | | |
| | | | C. B. Galloway[7] | Galloway | Galloway |
| | | | A. E. Orr[8] | Orr | Orr |
| | | | W. L. Wilson[9] | | |
| | | | B. Strong, *Clk.* | Strong, *Clk.* | Strong, *Sec.* |
| | | | | W. H. Baldwin, Jr.[10] | |

Appendix F

C. H. Dodge[11]
E. Capers[12]
S. Low[13]
W. Buttrick,[14]
*Genl. Agent*
W. T. B. Williams[15]
*School Visitor*

The following notes identify trustees and employees who either (1) died between 1891 and 1906, or (2) are *not* identified in the text.

[1] Died 1893.
[2] Died 1894.
[3] Died 1903.
[4] Died 1895.
[5] Died 1903.
[6] Governor of Georgia; elected trustee 1894, resigned 1899.
[7] Bishop, Methodist Episcopal Church, South.
[8] New York City public official; elected trustee 1895.
[9] U. S. Postmaster General, Member of Congress; President, Washington & Lee University; elected trustee 1895; died 1900.
[10] Railroad executive; elected trustee 1900, died 1905.
[11] Succeeded his father, W. E. Dodge, Jr., as trustee upon the latter's death in 1903.
[12] Of South Carolina; Bishop, Protestant Episcopal Church.
[13] President, Columbia University.
[14] Executive officer, General Education Board.
[15] Staff member, Hampton Institute, Hampton, Virginia.

*Appendix G*

## SLATER FUND GRANTS 1882-1891, 1895-1896

| School, Location, Affiliation | 1882-83 | 1883-84 | 1884-85 | 1885-86 | 1886-87 | 1887-88[4] | 1888-89 | 1889-90 | 1890-91 | 1891-92 | 1895-96[5] |
|---|---|---|---|---|---|---|---|---|---|---|---|
| 1. Clark University, Atlanta, Georgia, Methodist Episcopal Church. | $2,000 | | $2,000 | $1,400 | $1,400 | $2,150 (1,400) | $5,000 | $5,000 | $5,000 | $2,500 | |
| 2. Lewis High School, Macon, Georgia, American Missionary Association. | 200 | | | | | | | | | | |
| 3. Tuskegee Normal School, Tuskegee, Alabama, State. | 100 | $1,000 | 1,000 | | 1,000 | 1,000 (1,000) | 1,000 | 1,000 | 1,500 | 1,200 | $5,400 |
| 4. Tougaloo University, Tougaloo, Mississippi, American Missionary Association. | 1,000 | 1,000 | 1,000 | 1,000 | 1,500 | 1,500 (1,500) | 1,500 | 1,500 | 2,000 | 2,000 | 3,000 |
| 5. LeMoyne Institute, Memphis, Tennessee, American Missionary Association. | 500 | | 1,200 | 1,200 | 1,500 | 1,500 (1,500) | 1,300 | 1,300 | 1,300 | 1,300 | |
| 6. Claflin University, Orangeburg, South Carolina, Methodist Episcopal Church. | 2,000 | | 2,000 | 1,400 | 1,400 | 1,400 (1,400) | 1,800 | 1,800 | 2,000 | 2,000 | 4,000 |

*Appendix G*

## SLATER FUND GRANTS 1882-1891, 1895-1896 (Continued)

| School, Location, Affiliation | 1882-83 | 1883-84 | 1884-85 | 1885-86 | 1886-87 | 1887-88[4] | 1888-89 | 1889-90 | 1890-91 | 1891-92 | 1895-96[5] |
|---|---|---|---|---|---|---|---|---|---|---|---|
| 7. Atlanta University, Atlanta, Georgia, American Missionary Association. | 2,000 | 500 | 2,000 | 1,400 | 1,800 | 1,600 (1,400) | 1,600 | 1,600 | 1,600 | 2,000 | |
| 8. Talladega College, Talladega, Alabama, American Missionary Association. | 2,000 | | 2,000 | 1,400 | 1,400 | 1,400 (1,400) | 1,400 | 1,400 | 1,900 | 2,000 | 2,500 |
| 9. Shaw University, Raleigh, North Carolina, American Baptist Church. | 2,000 | | 2,000 | 1,800 | 1,800 | 1,800 (1,800) | 1,800 | 1,800 | 2,000 | 2,000 | 3,500 |
| 10. Hampton Institute, Hampton, Virginia, State, Federal (U. S.) | 2,000 | | 2,000 | 3,000 | 3,000 | 3,000 (3,000) | 2,500 | 2,500 | 2,500 | 2,500 | 6,000 |
| 11. Atlanta Baptist Female Seminary, Atlanta, Georgia, American Baptist Church. Name changed to Spelman Female Seminary,[1] (1884). | 2,000 | | 2,314 | 1,800 | 2,000 | 2,000 (2,000) | 2,000 | 2,000 | 2,500 | 2,500 | 5,000 |

Appendix G

| | | | | | | | | | | | |
|---|---|---|---|---|---|---|---|---|---|---|---|
| 12. Austin High School, Knoxville, Tennessee, Private/Public (City). Name changed to Slater Industrial School (1886), to Training School (1887). | 450 | | 500 | 500 | 600 | 600 (600) | 600 | 600 | 600 | | |
| 13. Brainerd Institute, Chester, South Carolina, Presbyterian Church in the U. S. A.. | | 750 | 500 | 500 | 500 | 700 (500) | 700 | 700 | 1,000 | 1,000 | |
| 14. Meharry Medical College, Nashville, Tennesee, Methodist Episcopal Church. | | 500 | 1,000 | 700 | 1,000 | 1,000 (1,000) | 1,000 | 1,000 | 1,200 | 1,200 | 1,500 |
| 15. Tillotson Institute, Austin, Texas, American Missionary Association. | | 600 | 600 | 600 | 600 | 900 (600) | 900 | 900 | 900 | 900 | |
| 16. Leonard Medical School, Raleigh, North Carolina, American Baptist Church. | | 500 | 1,000 | 500 | 500 | 500 (500) | 500 | 500 | 1,000 | 1,000 | |
| 17. Fisk University, Nashville, Tennessee, American Missionary Association. | | 1,975 | 2,000 | 1,300 | 1,300 | 1,300 (1,300) | 1,800 | 1,800 | 2,000 | 2,000 | |

*Appendix G*

## SLATER FUND GRANTS 1882-1891, 1895-1896 (Continued)

| School, Location, Affiliation | 1882-83 | 1883-84 | 1884-85 | 1885-86 | 1886-87 | 1887-88[4] | 1888-89 | 1889-90 | 1890-91 | 1891-92 | 1895-96[5] |
|---|---|---|---|---|---|---|---|---|---|---|---|
| 18. Central Tennessee College, Nashville, Tennessee, Methodist Episcopal Church. | | 500 | 1,500 | 1,100 | 1,100 | 1,100 (1,100) | 1,100 | 1,100 | 1,300 | 1,600 | |
| 19. Roger Williams University, Nashville, Tennessee, American Baptist Church. | | 1,350 | 1,400 | 1,000 | 1,000 | 1,000 (1,000) | 1,000 | 1,000 | 1,000 | 1,000 | |
| 20. Southern University, New Orleans, Louisiana, State. | | 250 | | | | | | | | | |
| 21. Leland University, New Orleans, Louisiana, American Baptist Church. | | 342 | 1,400 | 1,000 | 1,000 | 1,000 (1,000) | 1,000 | | | | |
| 22. Lincoln Normal University, Marion, Alabama, State. Name changed to Montgomery State Normal University and moved to Montgomery, Alabama, in 1888. | | 450 | 1,000 | 900 | 1,000 | 1,200 | 1,200 | 1,200 | 1,500 | 1,500 | 2,500 |

Appendix G

| | | | | | | | | | |
|---|---|---|---|---|---|---|---|---|---|
| 23. Rust University, Holly Springs, Mississippi, Methodist Episcopal Church. | 1,600 | | | 1,250 | 1,500 (1,500) | 1,100 | 1,100 | 1,300 | 1,300 |
| 24. Scotia Female Seminary, Concord, North Carolina, Presbtyerian Church in the U. S. A. | 240 | 1,000 | 700 | 700 | 700 (700) | 700 | 700 | 700 | 700 |
| 25. State Normal School, Huntsville, Alabama, State. | 1,000 | 1,000 | 600 | 700 | 700 (700) | | | | |
| 26. Kentucky Normal School, Louisville, Kentucky, American Baptist Church. | 1,000 | 1,000 | 700 | 700 | 700 (700) | | | | |
| 27. Hartshorn Memorial College, Richmond, Virginia, American Baptist Church. | 2,000 | 1,000 | 650 | 650 | 650 (650) | 650 | 650 | 650 | 650 |
| 28. Howard University, Washington, District of Columbia, Federal (U. S.) | 1,000 | 1,000 | 600 | 600 | 600 (600) | | | | |
| 29. Direct student aid (referred to in *The Proceedings* as "Special cases," "Special students," and "Special objects.") | 550 | 450 | 450 | 500 | 500 (500) | 500 | 500 | 500 | |

*Appendix G*

## SLATER FUND GRANTS 1882-1891, 1895-1896 (Continued)

| **School, Location, Affiliation** | 1882-83 | 1883-84 | 1884-85 | 1885-86 | 1886-87 | 1887-88[4] | 1888-89 | 1889-90 | 1890-91 | 1891-92 | 1895-96[5] |
|---|---|---|---|---|---|---|---|---|---|---|---|
| 30. Benedict Institute, Columbia, South Carolina, American Baptist Church. | | | 1,000 | 800 | 1,300 | 1,000 (1,000) | 1,000 | 1,000 | 1,000 | 1,000 | |
| 31. Lewis Normal Institute, Macon, Georgia, American Missionary Association. | | | 500 | 500 | 500 | 500 (500) | | | | | |
| 32. Mount Albion State Normal School, Franklinton, North Carolina, State. | | | 400 | 400 | 400 | 400 (400) | 400 | | | | |
| 33. Mount Hermon Female Seminary, Clinton, Mississippi, Private/non-denominational. | | | 1,000 | 1,000 | 1,000 | 1,000 (1,000) | 1,000 | 1,000 | 1,000 | 667 | |
| 34. Zion Wesley College, Salisbury, North Carolina, African Methodist Episcopal Church Zion. Name changed to Livingstone College in 1886. | | | | 200 | 800 | 700 (600) | 700 | 700 | 1,000 | 1,000 | |

Appendix G

| | | | | | | |
|---|---|---|---|---|---|---|
| 35. Beaufort Normal School, Beaufort, South Carolina, Presbyterian Church in the U. S. A. | 460 | 700 (700) | | | | |
| 36. Gilbert Seminary, Baldwin, Louisiana, Methodist Episcopal Church. | 500 | 500 (500) | 800 | 800 | 1,000 | 800 |
| 37. Jackson College, Jackson, Mississippi, American Baptist Church. | 700 | 800 (800) | 800 | 800 | 1,000 | 1,000 |
| 38. Moore Street Industrial School, Richmond, Virginia, Public. | 540 | 540 (540) | | | | |
| 39. New Orleans University,[2] New Orleans, Louisiana, Methodist Episcopal Church. | 600 | 1,000 (1,000) | 1,000 | 1,000 | 1,200 | 1,200 |
| 40. Paul Quin College, Waco, Texas, African Methodist Episcopal Church. | 300 | 460 (300) | 460 | 460 | 600 | 600 |
| 41. Paine Institute, Augusta, Georgia, Colored Methodist Episcopal Church/Methodist Episcopal Church, South. | 500 | 600 (600) | 600 | 600 | 600 | 600 |

*Appendix G*

## SLATER FUND GRANTS 1882-1891, 1895-1896 (Continued)

| **School, Location, Affiliation** | 1882-83 | 1883-84 | 1884-85 | 1885-86 | 1886-87 | 1887-88[4] | 1888-89 | 1889-90 | 1890-91 | 1891-92 | 1895-96[5] |
|---|---|---|---|---|---|---|---|---|---|---|---|
| 42. Philander Smith College, Little Rock, Arkansas, Methodist Episcopal Church. | | | | | 600 | 800 (800) | 800 | 800 | 1,000 | 600 | |
| 43. Rust Normal Institute, Huntsville, Alabama, Methodist Episcopal Church. | | | | | 300 | 300 (300) | | | | | |
| 44. Straight University, New Orleans, Louisiana, American Missionary Association. | | | | | 1,000 | 1,000 (1,000) | 1,300 | 1,300 | 1,500 | 1,500 | 1,000 |
| 45. Biddle University,[3] Charlotte, North Carolina, Presbyterian Church in the U. S. A. | | | | | | 1,200 | 1,000 | 1,000 | 1,000 | 600 | |
| 46. Jacksonville Grade School, Jacksonville, Florida, Public | | | | | | 1,000 (1,000) | 800 | 800 | 1,000 | 1,000 | |
| 47. Schofield Normal Institute, Aiken, South Carolina, Society of Friends. | | | | | | 500 | 500 | 500 | 1,000 | 1,000 | |

Appendix G

| | | | | | | | | | | | |
|---|---|---|---|---|---|---|---|---|---|---|---|
| 48. Ballard Normal School, Macon, Georgia, American Missionary Association. | | | | | | | 500 | 500 | 800 | 800 | |
| 49. Bishop College, Marshall, Texas, American Baptist Church. | | | | | | | | | | | 1,500 |
| TOTAL: | $16,250 | $17,107 | $36,764 | $30,000 | $40,000 | $45,000 ($40,390) | $44,310 | $42,910 | $49,650 | $45,217 | $35,900 |

[1] Named for Harvey B. Spelman, father-in-law of John D. Rockefeller, Sr., Cleveland merchant.
[2] Now part of Dillard University, New Orleans, Louisiana.
[3] Now Johnson C. Smith University, Charlotte, North Carolina.
[4] Figures in parentheses indicate amount budgeted by the Slater board's finance committee. The 1887-88 school year is the only one for which such figures were given in the board's *Proceedings*.
[5] Figures for 1895-96 are shown to illustrate changes in the Slater grants after a policy of concentration replaced the principle of diffusion.

*Appendix H*

## LETTER OF THE FOUNDER

To Messrs. Rutherford B. Hayes, of Ohio; Morrison R. Waite, of the District of Columbia; William E. Dodge, of New York; Phillips Brooks, of Massachusetts; Daniel C. Gilman, of Maryland; John A. Stewart, of New York; Alfred H. Colquitt, of Georgia; Morris K. Jesup, of New York; James P. Boyce, of Kentucky; and William A. Slater, of Connecticut:

Gentlemen, It has pleased God to grant me prosperity in my business, and to put into my power to apply to charitable uses a sum of money so considerable as to require the counsel of wise men for the administration of it.

It is my desire at this time to appropriate to such uses the sum of one million of dollars ($1,000,000); and I hereby invite you to procure a charter of incorporation under which a charitable fund may be held exempt from taxation, and under which you shall organize; and I intend that the corporation, as soon as formed, shall receive this sum in trust to apply the income of it according to the instructions contained in this letter.

The general object which I desire to have exclusively pursued, is the uplifting of the lately emancipated population of the Southern States, and their posterity, by conferring on them the blessings of Christian education. The disabilities formerly suffered by these people, and their singular patience and fidelity in the great crisis of the nation, establish a just claim on the sympathy and good will of humane and patriotic men. I cannot but feel the compassion that is due in view of their prevailing ignorance, which exists by no fault of their own.

But it is not only for their own sake, but also for the safety of our common country, in which they have been invested with equal political rights, that I am desirous to aid in providing them with the means of such education as shall tend to make them good men and good citizens—education in which the instruction of the mind in the common branches of secular learning shall be associated with training in just notions of duty toward God and man, in the light of the Holy Scriptures.

The means to be used in the prosecution of the general object above described, I leave to the discretion of the corporation; only indicating, as lines of operation adapted to the present condition of things, the training of teachers from among the people requiring to be taught, if, in the opinion of the corporation, by such limited selection the purposes of the trust can be best accomplished; and the encouragement of such institutions as are most effectually useful in promoting this training of teachers.

I am well aware that the work herein proposed is nothing new or untried. And it is no small part of my satisfaction in taking this share in it, that I hereby associate myself with some of the noblest of charity and humanity, and may hope to encourage the prayers and toils of faithful men and women who have labored and are still laboring in this cause.

I wish the corporation which you are invited to constitute, to consist at no time of more than twelve members, nor of less than nine members for a longer time than may be required for the convenient filling of vacancies, which I desire to be filled by the corporation, and, when found practicable, at its next meeting after the vacancy may occur.

I designate as the President of the corporation the Honorable Rutherford B. Hayes of Ohio. I desire that it may have power to provide from the income of the fund, among other things, for expenses incurred by members in the fulfillment of this trust, and for the expenses of such officers and agents as it may be necessary for carrying out the purposes of the trust. I desire, if it may be, that the corporation may have full liberty to invest its funds according to its own best discretions, without reference to or restriction by any laws or rules, legal or equitable, of any nature, regulating the mode of investment of trust funds; only I wish that neither principal nor income be expended in land or buildings for any other purpose than that of safe and productive investment for income. And I hereby discharge the corporation, and its individual members, so far as it is in my power to do so, all responsibility, except for the faithful understanding and best judgement. In particular, also, I wish to relieve them of any pretended claim on the part of any person, party, sect, institution or locality, to benefactions from this fund, that may be put forward on any ground whatsoever, as I wish every expenditure to be determined solely by the convictions of the corporation itself as to the most useful disposition of its gifts.

I desire that the doings of the corporation each year be printed and sent to each of the State Libraries in the United States, and to the Library of Congress.

In case the capital of the Fund should become impaired, I desire that a part of the income, not greater than one-half, be invested, from year to year, until the capital be restored to its original amount.

I purposefully leave to the corporation the largest liberty of making such changes in the methods of applying the income of the Fund as shall seem from time to time best adapted to accomplish the general object herein defined. But being warned by the history of such endowments that they sometimes tend to discourage rather than promote effort and self-reliance on the part of the beneficiaries; or to injure the advancement of learning instead of the dissemination of it; or to become a convenience to the rich instead of a help to those who need help; I solemnly charge my Trustees to use their best wisdom in preventing any such defeat of the spirit of this trust; so that my gift may continue to future generations to be a blessing to the poor.

If at any time after the lapse of thirty-three years from the date of this foundation it shall appear to the judgment of three-fourths of the members of this corporation that, by reason of a change in social condition, or by reason of adequate and equitable provision for public education, or for any other sufficient reason, there is no further serious need of this Fund in the form in which it is first instituted, I authorize the corporation to apply the capital of the Fund to the establishment of foundations subsidiary to the already existing institutions of higher education, in such wise as to make the educational advantages of such institutions more freely accessible to poor students of the colored race.

It is my wish that this trust be administered in no partisan, sectional or sectarian spirit, but in the interest of a generous patriotism and an enlightened Christian faith; and that the corporation about to be formed, may continue to be constituted of men distinguished either by honorable success in business or by services to literature, education, religion, or the state.

I am encouraged to the execution of this charitable foundation of a long-cherished purpose, by the eminent wisdom and success that has marked the conduct of the Peabody Education Fund in a field of operation not remote from that contemplated by this trust. I shall commit it to your hands, deeply conscious how insufficient is our best forecast for the future that is known only to God; but humbly hoping that the administration of it may be so guided by divine wisdom, as to be, in its turn, an encouragement to philanthropic enterprise on the part of others, and an enduring means of good to our beloved country and to our fellow-men.

I have the honor to be, Gentlemen, your friend and fellow-citizen.

JOHN F. SLATER

Norwich, Conn., March 4, 1882

Letter quoted in "Documents relating to the Origin and Work of the Slater Trustees," The Trustees of the John F. Slater Fund, *Occasional Papers,* No. 1 (1894), pp. 7-8.

# SELECTED BIBLIOGRAPHY

## PRIMARY SOURCES


### Books

Haygood, A. G. *Our Brother in Black.* Nashville: Southern Methodist Publishing House, 1881.

———. *Pleas for Progress.* Nashville: Southern Methodist Publishing House, 1889.

———. *Sermons and Speeches.* Nashville: Southern Methodist Publishing House, 1883.

### Pamphlets

Curry, J. L. M. "A Brief Sketch of George Peabody," Peabody Education Fund (1898).

———. "Difficulties, Complications, and Limitations Connected with the Education of the Negro," The Trustees of the John F. Slater Fund, *Occasional Papers,* No. 5 (1898).

"Documents Related to the Origin and Work of the Slater Trustees," The Trustees of the John F. Slater Fund, *Occasional Papers,* No. 1 (1894)

Gilman, Daniel C. "A Study in Black and White," The Trustees of the John F. Slater Fund, *Occasional Papers,* No. 10 (1897).

### Newspapers

*The Christian Advocate.* Nashville, Tennessee. Vols. XXXVIII (1878), XLIII (1883), L (1890), LI (1891).

*Wesleyan Christian Advocate.* Macon, Georgia. Vol. IV (1881).

### Miscellaneous

Haygood, A. G. "A Long and Weary March," Nashville *Christian Advocate.* Vol. LI (May 9, 1891).

———. *The Case of the Negro, As to Education in the Southern States: A Report to the Board of Trustees.* Atlanta: James P. Harrison & Co., 1885.

"Organization of the Trustees of the John F. Slater Fund for the Education of Freedmen," The Trustees of the John F. Slater Fund (1882).

Rubin, Louis D., Jr. (ed.). *Teach the Freeman: The Correspondence of Rutherford B. Hayes and the Slater Fund for Negro Education.* 2 vols. Baton Rouge: Louisiana State University Press, 1959.

Rutherford B. Hayes MSS. Rutherford B. Hayes Presidential Center, Fremont, Ohio.

The Slater Trustees *Proceedings,* 1883-1891, 1903.

Southern Education Foundation. *Annual Report,* 1983-84.

Williams. C. R. (ed.). *Diary and Letters of Rutherford Birchard Hayes: Nineteenth President of the United States.* 5 vols. Columbus: The Ohio State Archeological and Historical Society, 1922-1926.

## SECONDARY SOURCES

**Books**

Albright, Raymond Wolfe. *Focus on Infinity: A Life of Phillips Brooks.* New York: Seabury Press, 1964.

Brown, William Adams. *Morris Ketcham Jesup: A Character Sketch.* New York: Charles Scribner's Sons, 1910.

Butchart, Ronald E. *Northern Schools, Southern Blacks, and Reconstruction: Freedman's Education, 1862-1875.* Westport, CT: Greenwood Press, 1980.

The Commission on Foundations and Private Philanthropy, *Foundations, Private Giving and Public Policy.* Chicago: University of Chicago Press, 1970.

Cordasco, Francesco. *Daniel Coit Gilman and the Protean Ph.D.: The Shaping of American Graduate Education.* Leiden: E. J. Brill, 1960.

Cunninggim, Merrimon. *Private Money and Public Service.* New York: McGraw-Hill, 1972.

Dempsey, Elam F. *Atticus Greene Haygood.* Nashville: The Parthenon Press, 1939.

Eckenrode, Hamilton James. *Rutherford B. Hayes: Statesman of Reunion.* Port Washington, NY: Kenikat Press, 1963.

Flexner, Abraham. *Daniel Coit Gilman, Creator of the American Type of University.* New York: Harcourt, Brace & Company, 1946.

______. *Funds and Foundations.* New York: Harper & Brothers, 1952.

Gravely, William B. *Gilbert Haven, Methodist Abolitionist: A Study in Race, Religion, and Reform, 1850-1880.* Nashville: Abingdon Press, 1973.

Hollis, Ernest Victor. *Philanthropic Foundations and Higher Education.* New York: Columbia University Press, 1938.

Holmes, D. O. W. *The Evolution of the Negro College.* New York: Columbia University, 1934.

Johnson, Charles S. *The Negro in American Civilization.* New York: Henry Holt and Company, 1930.

Johnson, Gerald W. *American Heroes and Hero Worship.* New York: Harper & Brothers, 1943.

King, Willard Leroy. *Melville Weston Fuller, Chief Justice of the United States, 1888-1910.* New York: MacMillan, 1950.

Kurcher, Arnold J. *The Management of American Foundations.* New York: New York University Press, 1972.

Lowitt, Richard. *A Merchant Prince of the Nineteenth Century: William E. Dodge.* New York: Columbia University Press, 1952.

Magrath, Peter C. *Morrison R. Waite: The Triumph of Character.* New York: Macmillan, 1963.

Mann, Harold W. *Atticus Greene Haygood: Methodist Bishop, Editor and Educator.* Athens: University of Georgia Press, 1965.

Rice, Jessie Pearl. *J. L. M. Curry: Southerner, Statesman, and Educator.* New York: King's Crown Press, 1949.

Robertson, Archibald Thomas. *Life and Letters of John Albert Broadus.* Philadelphia: American Baptist Publication Society, 1901.

Spivey, Donald. *Schooling for the New Slavery: Black Industrial Education, 1868-1915.* Westport, CT: Greenwood Press, 1978.

Swint, H. L. *The Northern Teacher in the South, 1862-1870.* Nashville: Vanderbilt University Press, 1941.

Tarbell, Ida. *The Nationalizing of Business: 1878-1898.* Vol. IX of *A History of American Life.* Edited by Arthur M. Schlesinger and Dixon Ryan Fox. 12 vols. New York: The MacMillan Company, 1936.

Thomas, Benjamin P. *Abraham Lincoln.* New York: Alfred A. Knopf, 1952.

Trimble, Bruce Raymond. *Chief Justice Waite: Defender of the Public Interest.* Princeton: Princeton University Press, 1938.

Turner, Arlin. *George W. Cable, A Biography.* Baton Rouge: Louisiana State University Press, 1966.

Vaughn, William Preston. *Schools for All: The Blacks & Public Education in the South, 1865-1877.* Lexington: University of Kentucky Press, 1974.

**Unpublished Material**

Butler, John H. "An Historical Account of the John F. Slater Fund and the Anna T. Jeanes Foundation." Unpublished Ed.D. Thesis: University of California, 1931.

Finkenbine, Roy Eugene. "A Little Circle: White Philanthropists and Black Industrial Education in the Postbellum South." Unpublished Ph.D. Dissertation: Bowling Green State University, 1982.

Smith, Marion L. "Atticus Greene Haygood: Christian Educator." Unpublished Ph.D. Dissertation: Yale University, 1929.

**Newspapers**

*The Daily American.* Nashville, Tennessee. Vol. VIII (1883).

*The Daily Appeal.* Memphis, Tennessee. Vol. XLV (1885).

**Reports**

*Freedom to the Free: A Report to the President by the United States Commission on Civil Rights.* Washington: Government Printing Office, 1963.

*Report of the Commissioner of Education for the Year 1882-83.* Washington: Government Printing Office, 1884.

**Articles**

Filler, Louis. "Morrison R. Waite," *The Justices of the United States Supreme Court, 1789-1969; Their Lives and Major Opinions.* Edited by Leon Friedman and Fred L. Israel. Vol. II, 1969.

Schiffman, Irving. "Melville W. Fuller," *The Justices of the United States Supreme Court, 1789-1969; Their Lives and Major Opinions.* Edited by Leon Friedman and Fred L. Israel. Vol. II, 1969.

**Periodicals**

Cable, George W. "The Freedman's Case in Equity," *Century.* Vol. XXIX (January, 1885).

Davis, John W. "The Negro Land-Grant College," *Journal of Negro Education.* Vol. II (July, 1933).

Hill, Walter B. "Negro Education in the South," *Annals* of the American Academy of Political and Social Sciences, Vol. XXII, No. 2 (September, 1903).

Parker, Franklin. "George Peabody's Influence on Southern Educational Philanthropy," *Tennessee Historical Quarterly.* Vol. XX (March, 1961).

**Pamphlets**

Alexander, Will W. "The Slater and Jeanes Funds, An Educator's Approach to a Difficult Social Problem," The Trustees of the John F. Slater Fund, *Occasional Papers,* No. 28 (1934).

Brawley, Benjamin. "Early Efforts for Industrial Education," The Trustees of the John F. Slater Fund, *Occasional Papers,* No. 22 (1923).

Cable, George W. "The Negro Question," The American Missionary Association (1888).

Stewart, Maxwell S. "The Big Foundations," *Public Affairs Pamphlet,* No. 500 (1973).

Winton, George B. "A Life Sketch of Bishop A. G. Haygood," The Trustees of the John F. Slater Fund, *Occasional Papers,* No. 11 (1915).

**Miscellaneous**

*Appleton's Cyclopedia of American Biography.* Edited by J. G. Wilson and John Fiske. 8 vols. New York: D. Appleton & Company, 1887-1889 (Vol. 8 edited by J. E. Homans. Press Association, 1918).

"Catalog of the Officers and Students of Fisk University, Nashville, Tennessee, for 1895-1896," (1896).

*Dictionary of American Biography.* Edited by Allen Johnson, *et al.* 22 vols. 7 supplements. New York: Charles Scribner's Sons, 1928-1981.

*Federal Tax Guide, 1985.* Chicago: Commerce Clearing House, 1984.

*National Cyclopedia of American Biography.* 75 vols. New York: James T. White & Company, 1893-1984.

Renz, Loren (ed.). *The Foundation Directory.* 9th ed. New York: The Foundation Center, 1983.

# INDEX